The Ladysmith Siege.

2nd NOV., 1899—1st MARCH, 1900.

RECORD CONTAINING:

Regiments Defending the Besieged Borough.
Lists giving Names of Local Volunteer Defence Force.
Statistics.
The Residents: including Women and Children.
Copies of various Military and Municipal Notices.

AND A

Complete Copy of the "*Ladysmith Bombshell*" published during the Siege.

BY

G. W. LINES.

Dedicated to

JOSEPH FARQUHAR, ESQ.,

The first Mayor of the Borough of Ladysmith.

CONTENTS.

LADYSMITH: ITS ESTABLISHMENT IN 1851.

PARTICULARS OF THE MILITARY STAFF.

STRENGTH OF DEFENDING FORCES AT BEGINNING AND TERMINATION OF SIEGE.

REGIMENTAL STAFF.

AMMUNITION, CASUALTY, AND DISEASE STATISTICS.

BURIALS AT BOROUGH CEMETERY.

ALPHABETICAL LISTS, GIVING NAMES OF TOWN GUARD, INCLUDING RAILWAY AND CLIP RIVER RIFLE ASSOCIATIONS.

NAMES OF ALL BESIEGED BONA-FIDE RESIDENTS, INCLUSIVE OF WOMEN AND CHILDREN.

DISTINCT LIST OF N.G.R. EMPLOYEES.

INTOMBI CAMP NOTES.

COPY OF CERTAIN MILITARY AND MUNICIPAL NOTICES.

AND A COMPLETE COPY OF THE "LADYSMITH BOMBSHELL."

TOGETHER WITH ILLUSTRATIONS PUBLISHED THEREWITH.

LADYSMITH: ITS ESTABLISHMENT.

Collected and Arranged by G. W. LINES.

The Borough of Ladysmith (the Aldershot of South Africa) having the distinction of being the third largest town in the Colony, is situate 189¼ miles from the Port of Durban by rail, on the main road to Johannesburg, distant therefrom 290 miles, and 36 miles from the Orange Free State Border at Van Reenen.

It has a commonage of 16,887 acres 1 rood 29 perches, and is the seat of the Magistracy for the Klip River Division.

The township was first established in 1851 by the then Governor, Sir B. C. C. Pine. For the succeeding 30 years but little progress was made; it was not till the time of the Zulu and Transvaal wars that the town began to make headway. The settled prosperity of the Division became, however, due to the construction of the Government Railways. For a considerable period Ladysmith continued the terminus, during which time the greatest activity prevailed in the forwarding of goods and produce.

The Court House was erected in the year 1890, and the Town Hall and public offices in 1893.

Education is well provided for, there being the Government Primary Schools, the Convent, and two private schools, all of which are well attended.

The places of worship include the Church of South Africa (All Saints'), the Congregational, the Wesleyan, the Roman Catholic, and the Dutch Church, in addition to which the Lutheran Church is used for missions and prayer meetings. In St. John's Mission Station there is a church exclusively for Natives, and other denominations provide also for their religious instruction.

With the exception of the Gas Works, no other commercial undertaking in the town is carried on.

The water supply is obtained by means of gravitation from the Klip River. The cost of this important work was £25,000.

Ladysmith: Its Establishment.

There is a substantial bridge over the Klip River at the entrance to the town, erected in 1883 by the Government at a cost of £10,000.

The market for the sale of colonial produce is held twice a week.

There is a Public Reading Room and Library, which is extensively used.

Recently the Market Square Recreation Ground was entirely reformed, and a bicycle track added, with a length of 474 yards and a width of 21 feet. Every description of sport is well represented by the various clubs. To mark the year of Jubilee an ornamental Pavilion at a cost of about £650 was erected.

The Circuit Court is held four times a year.

A Sanatorium in connection with the Convent, which affords many advantages, has been completed, and arrangements for the reception of patients are now fully made.

This is an important postal and telegraphic centre. The District Engineer, the Public Works Department, and the District Natal Police have headquarters here. The Railway workshops give employment to a large number of mechanics.

In May, 1897, the military authorities entered into occupation of the upper portions of the Town Lands to the south of the Waterworks Reservoir, and it is conjectured, from the unusual advantages afforded, that this in future will be a permanent garrison town.

The population (excluding the military) comprises 2,200 Europeans, 1,200 Indians, and about 1,500 Natives. Judging from the amount of building still in progress, and the constant increase of the population, the town gives most favourable auguries of its future progress.

The memorable siege of 1899-1900 continued for a period of 120 days.

LIST CONTAINING FULL PARTICULARS OF MILITARY STAFF.

Rank and Name.		Appointment.
Lieut. General	Sir George S. White, V.C, G.C.B, G.C.S.I., G.C.I.E. ...	Commanding
PERSONAL STAFF.		
Colonel	B. Duff, C.I.E., I.S.C. ...	Asst. Military Sec.
Captain	F. Lyon, R.A. ...	A.D.C.
Lieutenant	E. C. Haag, 18th Hussars ...	A.D.C.
Captain	G. de H. Smith, I.S.C. ...	Orderly Officer
Major	F. Treherve, R.A.M.C. ...	Orderly Med. Officer
HEAD QUARTERS STAFF.		
Major General	Sir A. Hunter, K.C.B., D.S.O. ...	Chief of Staff
Major	A. J. King, Royal Lancaster Regiment ...	A.D.C.
Lieut. Colonel	Sir Henry S. Rawlinson, Bart. ...	A.A.G.
Lieut. Colonel	H. M. Lawson, R.E. ...	A.A.G.
Colonel	E. W. D. Ward, C.B. ...	A.A.G. (*b*)
Major	C. de C. Hamilton, R.A. ...	D.A.A.G.
Major	E. R. O. Ludlow, A.S.C. ...	D.A.A.G. (*b*)
Major	E. A. Altham, Royal Scots ...	A.A.G. Intelligence
Major	A. J. Murray, Royal Inniskilling Fusiliers ...	D.A.A.G. Intelligence
Major	D. Henderson, Argyll and Sutherland Highlanders ...	do.
Colonel	C. M. H. Downing, R.A. ...	Com. Royal Artillery
Captain	E. S. E. W. Russell, R.A. ...	Staff Captain R.A.
Colonel	R. Exham, R.A.M.C. ...	Prin. Med. Officer
Major	J. F. Bateson, R.A.M.C. ...	Sec. to Med. Officer
Vety. Lieut. Colonel	I. Matthews, A.V.D. ...	Prin. Vet. Officer
Captain	C. M. Dixon, 16th Lancers ...	Camp Commandant
Captain	F. A. B. Fryer, 6th Dragoons ...	Asst. Provost Marshal
Lieutenant	J. D. G. Walker, 2nd Royal Highlanders ...	Div. Signalling Officer
Major	W. F. Hawkins, R.E. ...	Director Telegraphs
Reverend	E. J. Macpherson ...	Sen. Chap., Ch. of E.
Reverend	T. Murray ...	do. Presby.

Military Staff—continued.

9

Reverend	O. S. Watkins	Sen. Chap., Wesleyan
Reverend	Father Ford	do. R. C.
Major	W. C. Savile, R.A.	Sen. Ordnce. Officer
Major	J. R. Dick	Field Paymaster
	CAVALRY BRIGADE.	
Major General	J. F. Brocklehurst, M.V.O.	Commanding
Lieutenant	Viscount Crichton, Royal Horse Guards	A.D.C.
Captain	G. P. Wyndham, 16th Lancers	Brigade Major
Captain	R. F. A. Sloane Stanley, 16th Lancers	Signalling Officer
Captain	E. S. E. Harrison, 11th Hussars	Galloper
	7th BRIGADE.	
Colonel	I. S. M. Hamilton, C.B., D.S.O.	Commanding
Lieutenant	B. H. H. Mathew-Launowe, 4th Dragoon Guards	A.D.C.
Captain	Earl of Eva (killed)	Orderly Officer
Captain	J. M. Vallentin, Somerset Light Infantry	Brigade Major
	8th BRIGADE.	
Major General	F. Howard, C.B., C.M.G., A.D.C.	Commanding
Captain	H. E. Vernon, D.S.O., Rifle Brigade	A.D.C.
Lieut. Colonel	Hon'ble C. G. Fortescue, Rifle Brigade	Brigade Major
Lieutenant	G. E. R. Kenrick, West Surrey Regiment	Signalling Officer
Captain	H. D'E. Vallancey, Argyll and Sutherland Highlanders	Asst. Provost Marshal
	DIVISIONAL TROOPS.	
Colonel	W. G. Knox, C.B.	Commanding
Major	H. Mullaly, R.E, to 12th December	D.A.A.G.
Major	H. Buchanan Riddell	
Lieut. Colonel	J. Stoneman, A.S.C.	D.A.A.G. (b)
Captain	J. R. Young, R.E.	Railway Staff Officer
Captain	V. S. Beves, Inniskilling Fusiliers	Remount Officer
	VOLUNTEER FORCE.	
Colonel	W. Royston	Commanding
Major	H. T. Bru de Wold	Chief Staff Officer
Major	J. Hyslop	Prin. Med. Officer

Military Staff—continued.

		Strength on 2nd November, 1899, commencement of Siege.								Guns		Casualties during Siege.								
	CORPS.	Effective		Sick and Wounded		Horses	Mules	Oxen	Attendants	Artillery	Machine	Killed		Wounded		Missing		Died of Wounds		Died of Disease	
		Officers	Men	Officers	Men							Officers	Men	Officers	Men	Officers	Men	Officers	Men	Officers	Men
1	5th (Princess Charlotte of Wales's) Dragoon Guards	29	486	...	6	518	175	...	60	...	1	...	1	3	8	...	...	...	...	1	29
2	5th (Royal Irish) Lancers	18	471	1	3	449	142	...	33	...	1	1	1	8	14	...	...	...	5	...	26
3	18th Hussars	22	413	...	2	335	132	...	34	...	1	...	4	1	25	...	...	...	2	2	8
4	19th (Princess of Wales's Own) Hussars	28	532	1	6	508	179	...	70	...	...	...	...	...	13	...	...	...	7	...	48
5	Imperial Light Horse	24	412	4	4	416	136	...	33	...	...	3	22	9	50	...	1	2	...	...	8
6	13th Battery Royal Field Artillery	5	172	...	2	140	28	...	9	6	...	...	...	...	4	...	...	...	...	...	5
7	21st " " " "	4	163	...	4	165	...	...	...	6	...	...	...	...	1	...	...	...	...	...	8
8	42nd " " " "	4	163	...	2	153	172	112	55	6	...	...	1	1	4	...	...	...	...	...	6
9	53rd " " " "	5	160	...	2	181	...	...	...	6	...	...	...	1	4	...	...	...	...	...	3
10	67th " " " "	5	164	...	1	144	28	...	7	6	...	...	...	1	1	...	...	...	...	...	4
11	69th " " " "	5	163	...	3	147	28	...	7	6	...	...	...	...	2	...	...	...	...	...	7
12	1st Brig. Div. Ammunition Column	4	102	1	1	79	114	90	38	...	...	...	...	...	...	...	...	...	...	...	3
13	2nd " " " "	3	98	...	1	143	Under	Bde. Div.	...	...	...	...	...	...	...	...	...	...	...	...	3
14	No. 10 Mountain Battery R.G.A.	1	85	...	5	9	142	...	81	2	...	...	1	...	6	...	...	...	1	...	...
15	Maxim Nordenfeldt Detachment	...	24	...	...	...	...	...	...	2	...	...	...	...	...	...	...	...	...	...	...
16	Howitzer Detachment	...	19	...	...	...	...	...	...	2	...	...	...	...	...	...	...	...	...	...	13
17	No. 23 Field Company Royal Engineers	6	189	...	2	26	64	...	21	...	...	2	7	...	9	...	...	...	...	...	3
18	Telegraph Battalion Royal Engineers	3	54	...	...	15	21	48	12	...	...	...	1	...	...	...	...	...	...	...	1
19	Balloon Section Royal Engineers	4	28	...	...	6	16	...	...	...	...	...	2	...	...	...	...	...	...	1	...
20	1st Battalion The King's (Liverpool Regiment)	26	879	...	...	127	198	...	47	...	1	...	2	...	16	...	...	...	5	...	31

Military Staff—continued.

#	Unit																			
21	1st Battalion Devonshire Regiment	27	824	1	4	7	190	52	...	1	4	18	9	43	...	...	...	1	5	20
22	1st ,, Leicestershire ,,	22	959	...	11	114	156	37	...	...	...	2	...	20	...	...	1	...	2	41
23	1st ,, Gloucestershire ,,	6	446	1	29	6	159	40	...	...	1	8	...	9	...	1	...	...	1	23
24	1st ,, King's Royal Rifle Corps	20	655	1	12	59	168	44	...	1	3	8	1	29	...	1	1	...	2	32
25	2nd ,, ,, ,, ,,	20	754	2	7	7	213	37	...	1	1	12	...	34	1	...	...	...	4	53
26	1st ,, Manchester Regiment	22	842	...	9	113	198	45	...	1	3	8	7	62	...	...	1	1	2	26
27	2nd ,, Gordon Highlanders	20	808	2	6	8	193	40	...	1	1	37	7	28	1	...	1	...	1	9
28	1st Battalion (Princess Victoria's) Royal Irish Fusiliers	8	230	2	20	6	65	18	...	1	...	15	4	7	1	...	1	...	...	10
29	Detachment 2nd Battalion Royal Dublin Fusiliers	3	55	1	2	1	...	...	...	...	2	1	...	...	...	...	...	...	...	1
30	2nd Battalion Rifle Brigade (The Prince Consort's Own)	23	755	...	3	8	169	43	...	1	...	33	9	85	...	...	6	3	8	29
31	Army Service Corps	5	96	...	...	6	...	...	...	...	...	...	2	...	...	...	1	...	...	4
32	Royal Army Medical Corps and Indian Field Hospitals	33	175	...	...	17	167	51	22	...	...	...	1	6	...	...	...	...	...	1
33	Army Ordnance Corps, No. 4 Co.	4	47	...	...	3	452	96	...	...	...	...	...	...	...	...	...	...	...	2
34	Indian Ordnance Department	4	15	...	...	3	462	976	...	4	...	2	2	6	...	...	3	...	...	20
35	Naval Brigade from H.M.S. *Powerful*	19	261	1	1	2	...	...	...	...	...	4	2	16	1	...	...	...	1	11
36	Volunteer Staff	23	48	...	...	40	30	119	...	2	...	2	2	3	...	...	...	1	...	3
37	Natal Carbineers	21	327	1	43	497	...	4	...	...	...	4	2	6	...	...	6	...	...	12
38	Natal Mounted Rifles	11	162	...	19	290	250	49	...	2	...	2	2	3	1	...	...	...	...	3
39	Border Mounted Rifles	10	238	1	19	334	...	...	...	...	...	4	1	6	...	...	...	...	...	4
40	Natal Police	2	71	...	...	76	...	2	...	2	...	1	...	3	...	...	...	...	...	1
41	Natal Naval Volunteers	3	64	...	...	1	6	...	...	...	...	2	...	1	...	...	...	...	...	3
42	Town Guard	...	120	...	...	...	...	2	...	...	...	...	...	...	...	...	...	...	...	...
43	Staff and Miscellaneous	70	200	...	...	150	41	13	...	...	...	3	6	3	...	...	...	...	...	...
44	Supply Columns	...	...	...	...	...	45	239	1429	...	...	...	...	...	...	...	...	...	...	...
45	In Store	...	...	...	...	...	...	...	...	...	...	...	...	...	4	...	...	...	...	...
	Civilians	...	...	...	...	...	...	...	...	...	...	1	...	7	...	...	...	2	...	12
	Followers	...	...	...	...	...	...	...	...	...	...	3	1	38	...	...	...	1	...	22
	Colt Gun Detachment	...	...	...	...	...	...	...	...	...	...	...	...	...	...	...	...	...	...	...
		572	12924	20	229	5309	4539	2412	1701	18	18	193	70	559	...	10	8	51	12	551

Military Staff—continued.

№	Effective Officers	Effective Men	Sick and Wounded Officers	Sick and Wounded Men	Horses	Mules	Oxen	Attendants	Guns Artillery	Guns Machine	Commander	Adjutant
1	18	354	8	106	73	112		39		1	Lieut. Col. St. J. C. Gore	Lieut. W. O. Winwood
2	11	349	7	97	168	138		37		1	Lieut. Col. J. F. M. Fawcett	Lieut. H. H. Hulse
3	15	356	7	42	252	118		36			Major E. C. Knox	Captain Hon. H. S. Davey
4	15	341	12	147	86	120		50			Lieut. Col. C. B. H. Wolseley-Jenkins	Lieut. M. Archer Shee
5	16	213	12	164	291	163		39			Lieut. Col. A. H. M. Edwards	Lieut. P. D. Fitzgerald, 11th Hussars
6	5	150		19	80	23		7	6		Major J. W. G. Dawkins	
7	3	123	1	36	95				6		Major W. E. Blewitt	
8	4	117		42	117	133	64	59	6		Major C. E. Goulburn	
9	3	117	2	41	102				6		Major A. J. Abdy	
10	4	134	1	27	88	26		7	6		Major J. F. Manifold	
11	2	138	3	21	55	35		10	6		Major F. D. V. Wing	
12	4	80		20	29	82	48	35			Major E. S. May	
13	1	78	2	13	75	Under Bde. Div.					Captain R. G. Ouseley	
14	1	72	1	14	7	75		57	2		Captain T. R. C. Hudson	
15	1	22		2	1	13		1	2		Lieut. K. G. Kincaid-Smith	
16	2	18		1	1			4	2		Captain H. W. A. Christie	
17	4	139		31	30	62		24			Captain G. H. Fowke	
18	3	43		8	14	5		12			Major W. F. Hawkins	
19	4	19		7	8	16					Major G. M. Heath	
20	20	656	5	185	32	198		42		1	Lieut. Col. L. S. Mellor	Lieut. L. M. Jones

Strength at Termination of Siege, 1st March, 1900.

Military Staff—continued.

No.										Name	Name
21	17	714	6	71		172			1	Lieut. Col. C. W. Park	Captain H. S. L. Ravenshaw
22	17	761	4	164	77	133			1	Lieut. Col. G. D. Carleton	Captain H. L. Croker
23	5	371	2	72	7	59				Captain C. J. Venables	Lieut. C. J. Hickie
24	16	490	4	131	39	127			1	Lieut. Col. Gore Browne	Captain H. R. Blore
25	17	499	2	196	7	130				Colonel G. G. Grimwood	Lieut. H. C. R. Green
26	16	629	6	156	34	180			1	Lieut. Col. A. E. R. Curran	Captain W. P. E. Newbigging
27	15	729	5	60	10	165		42	1	{ Lt. Col. Dick Cunyngham, V.C. (Lieut. Col. Scott from Jan. 7) }	Captain E. Streatfield
28	3	186	7	53	3	60		19	1	Brevet Major D. W. Churcher	Lieut. P. Gould
29	1	43	3	13	7	128		39		Lieut. H. W. Higginson	
30	14	537	4	145	10	140		48	1	Lieut. Col. C. T. E. Metcalfe	Lieut. Hon. H. Dawnay
31	4	81		10	1	253	44	37		Colonel E. W. D. Ward, C.B.	
32	18	160	12	14	22	384	46	951		Colonel R. Exham	Major J. F. Bateson
33	4	37		8	4					Major W. C. Savile, R.A.	
34	4	14		1	3	17		119		Major R. H. Mahon, R.A.	
35	13	205	5	32	2			4	4	Captain Hon. H. Lambton, R.N.	
36	17	17		31	58						
37	15	149	6	206	427			50	2	Colonel W. Royston	Major H. T. Bru de Wold
38	6	106	6	70	158	237					
39	5	116	5	125	288			6	2		
40	2	32	5	35	37					Colonel J. G. Dartnell, C.M.G.	
41	3	52		6	2			13		Commander Tatum	
42		119	10			43	50	287		Captain Molyneux	
43	55	195		2	100	166			4		
44		In use									
45											
	403	9761	154	2624	2907	3713	252	2302	55		
									18		

Military Staff—continued.

STRENGTH SUMMARY.

When.	Effective.		Sick and Wounded.		Horses.	Mules.	Oxen.	Attendants.	Guns.	
	Officers.	Men.	Officers.	Men.					Artillery.	Machine.
On 2nd November, 1899 ...	572	12924	20	229	5309	4539	1701	2412	55	18
On 1st March, 1900 ...	403	9761	154	2624	2907	3713	252	2302	55	18

AMMUNITION STATISTICS.

DESCRIPTION.

	4·7-in. Naval.	12-lb. Naval.	6·3-in. Howitzer.	15-lb.	9-lb.	2·5-in.	Maxim Nordenfelt	Hotch-kiss.	·303.	Pistol.
On hand 2nd November, 1899 ...	556	1036	887	11437	208	2417	189	1567	5678716	98149
Expended during Siege ...	514	784	776	3705	25	101	48	80	213400	...
Balance 1st March, 1900 ...	42	252	111	7732	183	2316	141	1487	5465316	98149

CASUALTY LIST.

	Killed.		Wounded.		Missing.		Died of Wounds.		Died of Disease.	
	Officers.	Men.	Officers.	Men.	Officers.	Men.	Officers.	Men.	Officers.	Men.
Total during Siege ...	18	193	70	559	...	10	8	51	12	529*
Due to Assaults, Sorties, &c. ...	17	160	45	352	...	7	6	35	...	...
Due to Casual Bombardment ...	1	33	25	207	...	3	2	16	...	...

* 22 followers also died.

DISEASE STATISTICS.

	Total Admissions and Deaths.		Enteric.		Dysentery.		Wounds.		Other Causes.	
	Admissions.	Deaths.	Admissions.	Deaths.	Admissions.	Deaths.	Admissions.	Deaths.	Admissions.	Deaths.
During Siege ...	10688	600	1766	393	1857	117	524	59	6541	31

LADYSMITH TOWN GUARD.
Organised as a Volunteer Defence Force.

DIVISIONAL UNITS.
1. Ladysmith Town Guard Rifle Association.
2. Klip River Rifle Association.
3. N.G. Railway Rifle Association.

OFFICERS OF COMBINED GUARD.
Dec. 12 to Dec. 22, Officer Commanding, Capt. J. R. Young, R.E.

Dec. 23, to Mar. 1, Officer Commanding, Capt. Molyneux, Natal Volunteer Staff.

Adjutant, R. A. L. Brandon.

OFFICERS OF UNITS.

Ladysmith Town Guard, R.A.
President	Joseph Farquhar (Mayor).
Secretary and Treasurer ...	G. W. Lines.
Assistant do.	R. A. L. Brandon.
Leader Ward 1	W. G. Hiscock.
,, ,, 2	R. S. C. Walker.
,, ,, 3	C. J. Jones.
Sub-Leader Ward 1	J. R. Bayley.
,, ,, 2	J. Baldock.
,, ,, 3	F. S. Ralfe.

Klip River, R.A.
Vice-President	W. Adams.
Sub-Leader	W. Steele.

N.G. Railway R.A.
President	E. Hacker.
Sub-Leader	F. Binnie.

WARD 1.

Bayley, James Robert
Brazier, Charles
Bulleier, John Joseph
Cameron, Edward
Carter, Herbert
Coventry, Richard
De Barry, Frederick
Davies, James Eaton
Davies, Walter Edward
Dahl, Edward

Dunkley, George
Dunkley, Henry John
Dimmock, George
Haden, Lewis
Hiscock, William G.
Horsley, Reginald Richard
Honey, John
Lenthall, Claude Hamilton
Lines, George Walter
Lloyd, Hy. Charles

Town Guard—continued.

Mercer, Herbert
Pearce, Charles Henry
Pattinson, Joseph
Roberts, Richard Gilbert
Turner, Thos. Edward
Walker, James
Wright, Alfred

WARD 2.

Brandon, Rupert Augustus Lacy
Baldock, John
Buchan, James
Cowan, George
Cowan, John Alexander
Ellison, George
Ellison, Thomas
Fowlds, William (died during siege)
Leonard, Richard Pearse
Mahon, Ernest Percival
Mahon, Alfred Joseph
Reed, George Richard
Roberts, David
Sahlstrom, Martin Oscar
Sorsen, John
Walker, Robert Selby Clarke
Wright, William John

WARD 3.

Adam, James Mills
Bewick, Robert Walker
Crouch, Henry
Cowan, Robert
Clifford, Montague
Cairns, Thomas
Doig, Alexander Henry
Dunton, Alfred John
Davenport, Frank
Farquhar, Joseph
Francis, Alfred Ella
Friggens, Ed. Jno.
Fraser, George
Fraser, Simon
Graham, Robert
Gourlay, Alexander
Glente, John Henry
Hewitt, Thos. Solomon
Harvey, Leonard
Hutchinson, Guy
Hyde, Henry Osmond
Hunter, William Young
Jones, Charles James
Jones, Walter William
Johnson, George Henry
Kelly, Frank Joseph
Leece, John
Leonard, Louis Augustus
Moffatt, James Ebenezer
Marlor, Frederick Harwood
MacPherson, Alexander
MacPherson, William
MacKay, Chas. Sinclair
McBlaine, John
Osborn, John
Ralfe, Francis Stewart
Ruddock, Thos. Victor
Russell, George Lauder
Stephenson, James
Surgeson, Joseph B.
Treadway, John Joseph
Thompson, Alexander Guthrie
Thomson, George
Thomson, William
Walters, Frederick James
Williams, Charles
Ward, Walter William
Webster, Thos. Edmondstone

Note.—Ward 3 also included Ward 4.

Town Guard—*continued.*

KLIP RIVER RIFLE ASSOCIATION.

Adams, William
Adams, John Henry
Allsopp, Leonard Webster John
Arbuckle, Alexander (died during siege)
Brookes, John Arthur
Brookes, Thomas
Brockbank, William
Coventry, Charles
Harburn, Christopher Richard
Horsley, Frederick Lovell
Kendall, Thos. Frederick
Moll, Robert Macfarlane
Malcolm, Alexander
Norris, Alfred William
Newton, James Hope
Pearson, Henry Hooke
Pinkney, George
Porter, Francis Noble Liston
Robinson, George Edgecumbe, junr.
Russell, George William Bishop
Steele, William
Thornhill, George Henry
Turner, Henry Augustus
Watson, William Tottie
Wills, Joseph Bain
Young, Frank

N. G. RAILWAY RIFLE ASSOCIATION.

Allen, Joseph
Binnie, Francis
Bottomley, Edward Alfred Taylor
Baillie, Ronald
Burleigh, James George
Clarke, Edward William
Clarke, William
Collingham, John Christopher
Croshaw, Frederick William
Curry, William Francis
Filler, Robert George
Frere, Gerald Hanbury
Gilkes, Charles
Goodman, Bernard
Gourlay, George
Gourlay, William
Hacker, Edward
Hillstrom, H. B.
Hinchcliff, Mark
Hutchinson, John
Hey, George
Hamber, Percy Douglas
Hilder, John Edward James
Holland, Andrew William
Kinnear, Alexander Gordon
Kirk, Robert John Stephenson
Last, Ernest James
Lee, Arthur Charles
Mellis, Walter Frederick William
Munro, Alexander
Perfect, Henry Edward
Perfect, Alfred James
Prangley, Ferdinand Alexander
Ramage, Thos. Trotter
Robinson, Gray William
Sayers, Andrew William
Slade, Albert William
Sinclair, Chas. (died during siege)
Smith, William Henry
Swan, Andrew
Todd, Cedric Valentine (died during siege)
Tourle, Albert

ALPHABETICAL LIST OF BESEIGED RESIDENTS.

(This does not include members of Town Guard, Railway, and Klip River Rifle Associations).

A.

Adams, A., Chemist
Allsopp, Mrs. L. W. J.
Allsopp, Gertrude E. M.
Allsopp, Leonard V.
Allsopp, Arthur H.
Allsopp, Lynett D.
Ahnert, Herman, Car Proprietor
Anders, T. A., Engineer
Anderson, J. G., Doctor
Anderson, Mrs. J. (Lyle Street)
Andersson, R. C., Surveyor
Angus, W., Brickmaker
Arbuckle, Mrs. A.
Arbuckle, Elsie
Arbuckle, May
Ayson, N. W., Standard Bank Clerk

B.

Bainbridge, John, M.L.A
Bainbridge, Mrs. J.
Brazier, Mrs. C.
Baldock, Mrs. John
Baldock, David
Baldock, Esther
Baldock, Francis
Baldock, Jonathan
Baldock, Edith
Baldock, Evelyn
Banbury, W., Builder and Contractor
Barker, Archdeacon
Barker, Mrs.
Barker, Edith
Barker, Olive
Blane, Mrs. W. M.
Brooke, F. W., P.W.D.
Brown, Matthew, Farmer
Brown, Mrs. M.
Brown, M., Jun.
Boyd, J. Lyle, Saddler's Manager
Brandon, R. A. L., Chief Clerk (Court House)
Buddle, J., Contractor
Buddle, Mrs. J.
Bush, Miss Doris, Organist
Butler, J., Blacksmith and Farrier
Brockbank, Mrs. W.
Brockbank, W. Walton
Brockbank, Cecil Saxelby
Brockbank, Jno. Munroe
Button, Frank, Produce Dealer

C.

Cairns, James, Builder and Contractor
Carde, Mrs.
Carter, Mrs. A.
Carter, Jessie
Carter, May
Carter, Stanley
Cawood, Rev. S. B., Wesleyan Minister
Charlton, R., Engineer
Charlton, Mrs. R.
Charlton, Caroline

Charlton, Ethel
Charlton, Edgar
Charlton, George
Chisnall, Richard, Hotel Proprietor
Chisnall, Mrs. R.
Chisnall, Beatrice
Chisnall, Ada
Chisnall, William
Clark, Mrs. F. H.
Clark, Jessie G.
Clarke, Mrs. H. A.
Clarke, Burchmore
Clegg, T., Mineral Water and Ice Manufacturer
Cormac, Mrs.
Cormac, Grace
Cormac, Jessie
Cormac, George
Cox, R.
Crownie, H., Violinist
Cowan, Mrs. R.
Cowan, Ivy
Cowan, Jane
Cowan, Mary
Cowan, George
Cowan, Maud
Cowan, Natalie
Corker, E. W., Hotel Waiter
Corker, J. D., Hotel Waiter
Craddock, J. B., Acting Postmaster
Cumming, S. G., Mill Manager
Cunningham, J. P. Grey, Dentist
Cunningham, Mrs. J. P. Grey
Cunningham, Cicely N.
Cunningham, Kathleen M.
Cunningham, Norah D.

D.

Dahl, E., Painter
Davidson, Mrs. G.
Davidson, Mary
Davies, Mrs. J. E., seriously injured by shell
De Lease, Mrs. John
De Lease, Alice
De Lease, Juliet
De Lease, Robert
De Lease, Rose, died during siege
Doig, Mrs. A. H.
Doig, Lilian
Dorehill, W. V., Inspector N.P.
Dunkley, Mrs.
Dunkley, Miss
Dyson, Joe, Night Auctioneer
De Ross, Mrs. W.

E.

Ellis, S., Store Manager
Ellison, Joseph, Brickmaker

F.

Farquhar, Joseph, first Mayor of Ladysmith
Forbes, Mrs. John
Forbes, Annie
Forbes, Bella, died during siege
Forbes, James
Forbes, John, junr.
Forbes, Lizzie
Forbes, Mary
Forbes, Christiana, born and died during siege
Foss, H. C., Miller

Residents—*continued.*

Foster, Mrs.
Foster, Percy, Storeman
Fowlds, Mrs. W.
Fowlds, Jerry
Fowlds, Maria
Fowlds, Stephen
Francis, Mrs. A. E.
Francis, Edward G. H.
Francis, Jas. W.
Francis, Wm. T.
Francis, May Frances
Francis, J. T., Auctioneer
Francis, Mrs. J. T.
Francis, Basil
Francis, Alma
Francis, Clavis
Francis, Grace
Francis, Olive

G.

Gibson, George, Hotel Manager
Gibson, Mrs. G.
Gibson, Amy E.
Gibson, Daisy L.
Gibson, G. A. J.
Giles, Douglas G., Acting Magis- [trate
Gillon, Miss
Gradwell, Mrs. S. W.
Gradwell, Mabel
Gradwell, Margaret
Gradwell, William
Greening, Thomas, Printer

H.

Haden, Mrs.
Hadden, J., Stonemason
Hamp, W. T., Chemist's Manager
Harburn, Mrs. C. R.
Harburn, Chris. D.
Harburn, Arthur G.
Harburn, E. Maud
Harburn, Wilfrid W.
Harburn, Vera
Harper, Mrs.
Harper, Miss
Hepworth, Mrs.
Hepworth, Agnes
Hepworth, Albert
Hepworth, James
Hepworth, John
Hepworth, Wilhelmina
Hayburn, F. S., Post Office Clerk (taken prisoner by Boers in attempting to cross their lines)
Honey, R. J., Post Office Clerk
Horsley, Francis S.
Horsley, Ada G.
Horsley, John [ant
Hutchinson, John, Store Assist-
Hutchinson, Robert, Store Assistant
Horsley, Mrs. F.

I.

Illing, Herman, Storekeeper
Illing, W. A., Storekeeper
Ingram, G. H., P.W.L.

J.

Jacobs, H. A., Platelayer
Jacobs, Mrs. H. A.
Jacobs, Fred
Jacobs, Bella
Jones, W. W., Butcher

Residents—*continued*.

K.

Keith, J., Agent
King, Robert, P.W.D. Engineer
Kirk, R. J. S.
Kisch, Henry, Photographer
Kisch, Harold, Clerk

L.

Lotter, J., Gaoler

M.

Mackrill, P., Tailor
Mackrill, Mrs. P.
Mackrill, Claris
Mackrill, Audley
Magee, F. F., Boarding House Keeper
Malcolm, W., Contractor
Marshall, H., Agent and Store Manager
Martin, A. H., Trolley Proprietor
Mellis, Mrs. G. H. R.
Mellis, G. H. R., no occupation
Mellis, Rosey
Miller, Joseph, Controller of Rations issued to the besieged inhabitants
Miller, Mrs.
Miller, Ethel
Miller, Gertrude
Miller, Maud
Miller, R. E.
Miller, Matilda
Miller, Ethel
Miller, Lizzie
Miller, Willie
Miller, W. H., Sergt. N. Police
Murray, John, Club Proprietor
Murray, Mrs. J.
Moor, E. B., Farmer
Moss, C. H., Storeman
Masterman, Mrs. J. T.
Masterman, Ethel
Masterman, Florence

Mc.

McAdam, T.
McAdam, Miss
McBeath, A., Assistant Police Officer
MacDonald, Wm., Chief Borough Police
McNellan., W., Plumber
McPherson, John, Store Assistant

N.

Nicholson, Mrs. E.
Norris, Mrs. A. W.
Norris, Elizabeth N.

O.

O'Connor, J., Hotel Assistant
Osborne, G., Mason
Osborne, G. A.

Residents—*continued.*

P.

Pain, Mrs. F.
Payne, H. G., Builder
Payne, Mrs. H. G.
Payne, Harold
Payne, Henry
Payne, Albert
Payne, Hilda
Payne, Ida
Payne, Maud
Payne, Muriel
Payne, William
Phillips, Edward, Solicitor
Prangley, Marshall
Prangley, Emily
Powell, John, Nurseryman
Procter, H. C., Doctor
Pattinson, Mrs. J.
Price, Mrs. G.
Price, Herbert G. C.

R.

Ramage, J. M., Store Assistant
Reid, R. J., Overseer
Reid, Mrs. R. J.
Reid, Albert
Reid, Arthur
Reid, Cyril
Reid, Isabel
Reid, James
Reid, Maud
Reid, William
Riddell, Jock, Tailor
Roberts, Richard, Dutch Interpreter
Robertson, Alec, Stonemason
Rouillard, A. A., Doctor
Russouw, Mrs.
Russouw, Charles
Russouw, Fritz
Russouw, John
Russouw, Rayner
Roux, P. R., Chemist's Assistant
Ruiter, P., Cemetery Custodian

S.

Salmond, W., Doctor (partly occupied in Intombi camp)
Scott, James, Auctioneer and Conveyancer
Sharratt, Ernest
Shirley, T. E., Army Contractor
Smith, J. W., Hotel Assistant
Snowball, Miss, Milliner
Sternberg, Freddie
Sternberg, Mrs.
Sternberg, Willie
Stevenson, Mrs. James
Stevenson, Archie
Stevenson, Maggie
Stevenson, James, junr.
Stevenson, Jessie
Stevenson, Rachael
Steele, Mrs. W., partly in residence
Steele, Christina T., partly in residence
Steele, Maggie D., partly in residence
Stewart, William, Tailor
Stewart, Mrs. W.
Stewart, Vivian R. S.
Stewart, Lydia
Stewart, Margaret (died during siege)
Spearman, Arthur, Store Assistant
Spearman, Ernest, Store Assistant
Sunberg, Mrs. R., Restaurant Keeper
Sutton, S. W., Army Contractor

Residents—continued.

T.

Tapp, F. H., Congregational Minister
Tatham, Mrs. G. F.
Teesdale, W. J., Accountant
Teesdale, Mrs. W. J.
Thompson, Mrs., Librarian
Thompson, Annie
Thompson, Charlie
Thompson, Elizabeth
Thomson, C., Congregational Minister
Thornhill, Alice
Thornhill, Francis
Thorrold, Sydney, Butcher (safely made his way through Boer lines for Durban)

V.

Verster, Mrs., senr.

W.

Walker, Mrs. R. S. C.
Walker, Ethel
Walker, Florence
Walker, Lilian
Walker, Queenie
Walker, Daisy [siege]
Walker, Patience (born during
Walker, James, Salesman
Watson, W., no occupation
Watson, Miss F.
Watson, Mrs. W. T.
Watson, Daisy O. R.
Watson, Colin C. H.
Watson, Laura Z.
Watson, Mary E.
Webber, Henry, Stonemason
Webber, Annie
Webber, Nellie
Webber, Mrs. H. (died during siege)
Wetherill, Mrs., senr.
Willis, G. W., Law Agent
Willis, Mrs. G. W.
Willis, Harry Buller Siege (born during siege)
Willis, Hettie Emily
Willis, Marie
Willis, Marius C.
Willis, Violet M. C.
Wright, Mrs. G. (overtown)
Wright, Mrs. D. C.
Wright, Ada
Wright, Ada
Wright, David
Wright, Mary
Wright, Sarah A.
Wright, Wm. C.
Wright, Arthur
Wright, John
Wright, Mrs. W. J.
Wright, Kate
Wright, Harry
Wright, Alfred
Wright, W. (Colworth), Farmer
Wright, Daisy, late "Arcadia"
Wright, Florence, late "Arcadia"
Wright, Harriet, late "Arcadia"
Wright, Isabel, late "Arcadia"
Wright, Laura, late "Arcadia"
Wood, H. E., Brewery Agent

NATAL GOVERNMENT RAILWAY EMPLOYEES.

N. G. Railway employees on duty during siege (in addition to Railway Rifle Association):—

Alsop, C. (Loco.)
Angus, H. (Main.)
Axtelius, A. (Loco.)
Anderson, J. (Loco.)
Butler, T. A. (Traffic)
Brown, W. (Main.)
Burgess, H. (Loco.)
Boyle, G. (Loco.)
Campbell, H. (Traffic)
Callingham, C. (Traffic)
Crowe, W. H. (Traffic)
Cresswell, H. (Traffic)
Cormac, R. (Traffic)
Connelly, J. (Traffic)
Clarke, F. H. (Traffic)
Carpenter, C. (Main.)
Crosley, John (Loco.)
Cathro, R. (Loco.)
Collins, J. (Loco.)
Dermott, F. (Traffic)
Dempster, H. (Traffic)
Dilworth, J. (Traffic)
Dawes, E. (Traffic)
Doull, H. M. (Main.)
De Ross, W. (Main.)
Douglas, D. (Main.)
Eagle, W. (Traffic)
Ellwood, W. (Traffic)
Edwards, W. (Traffic)

Ellis, F W. (Traffic)
Ellis, J. (Loco.)
Eschenhoff, G. (Loco.)
Forge, W. (Traffic)
Foley, J. (Traffic)
Fletcher, F. C. (Main.)
Fegan, P. (Loco.)
Fraser, E. (Loco.)
Fletcher, J. (Loco.)
Gardner, R. (Loco.)
Grievson, W. (Loco.)
Heher, C. G. (Traffic)
Harvard, F. (Main.)
Hayes, H. (Loco.)
Hargreaves, J. (Loco.)
Hibberd, C. (Loco.)
Heward, W. (Loco.)
Hepworth, J. (Loco.)
Hodginson, F. (Loco.)
Ingoldsby, T. (Traffic)
Jury, D. (Traffic)
Jackson, W. (Loco.)
Jacobson, C. (Loco.)
Jackson, C. (Loco.)
Kinghorn, A. (Main.)
Lamont, A. (Traffic)
Laverton, W. (Main.)
Laverton, A. (Main.)
Lusted, H. (Loco.)

Besieged Residents—continued.

Mellis, W. H. (Traffic)
Mills, J. (Traffic)
Morton, James (Traffic)
Masterman, J. (Traffic)
Miller, W. G. (Traffic)
MacArthur, G. (Main.)
MacBain, A. (Main.)
Medcalf, J. D. (Main.)
Mackanlay, A. (Loco.)
Mallandain, E. (Loco.)
Martin, J. (Loco.)
Martin, L. (Loco.)
Massey, W. (Loco.)
Miller, R. (Loco.)
Miller, W. T. (Loco.)
Neath, J. W. (Traffic)
Neil, R. (Loco.)
Prangley, J. E. (Traffic)
Porter, H. (Traffic)
Pope, R. (Traffic)
Pilkenrood, H. J. (Traffic)
Powell, J. (Traffic)
Payne, H. (Main.)
Porter, Horace (Loco.)
Parker, J. (Loco.)
Price, G. (Loco.)
Russell, J. R. (Traffic)
Robson, W. (Main.)
Roberts, T. (Main.)
Roberts, E. H. (Main.)
Ritson, H. J. (Loco.)
Richards, S. (Loco.)
Rayner, P. (Loco.)
Smith, S. (Traffic)
Stracham, A. (Traffic)
Simmonds, E. (Traffic)
Shaw, M. (Main.)
Sheriff, W. (Main.)
Spence, D. S. (Main.)
Spencer, Walter (Loco.)
Stracham, J. (Loco.)
Stead, A. (Loco.)
Spencer, H. (Loco.)
Sumner, W. (Loco.)
Scott, S. (Loco.)
Thorburn, J. (Station master, Harrismith)
Thompson, W. (Loco.)
Waterhouse, J. (Traffic)
Weston, H. J. (Traffic)
Wooster, A. E. (Traffic)
Wegner, B. (Traffic)
Watt, J. (Main.)
Walkden, P. (Main.)
Watts, W. (Loco.)
Wanblad, A. (Loco.)
Young, G. (Main.)

The Editor much regrets that in consequence of the disastrous fire at his Publishers' premises, wherein a considerable quantity of manuscript was destroyed, it is impossible to reproduce the list of the Refugees (giving some 700 names) together with the list of Residents and others, who took shelter at Intombi Camp.

BURIALS AT BOROUGH CEMETERY.

A.

Name.	Date Buried.			No. of Grave.	Section.
Alofson, N.	Oct,	27,	1899	2, L	A x 1
✓ Adams, Lieut. (I.L.H.)	Jan.	7,	1900	19, L	B x 2
Ava, Lord	,,	11,	,,	31, R	S 1
Allison, James (baby)	,,	14,	,,	5, R	x 3
Arnold, Pte. (Leicesters)	,,	17,	,,	1, L	C x 2
Agnew, Victor S.	,,	25,	,,	12, R	x 4
Arbuckle, Alex.	Feb.	20,	,,	14, L	C 2

B.

Name.	Date Buried.			No. of Grave.	Section.
Bradbury, Lieut. (Gordons)	Oct.	23,	1899	33, R	x 2
Boers (Three)	,,	24,	,,	1	{ A x 3 A x 2 A x 1
,, (One)	,,	24,	,,		A x 3
,, (Two)	,,	24,	,,	7	A x 3
,, (One)	,,	27,	,,	2, L	A x 2
Brown, Samuel (Volunteers)	,,	26,	,,	29, R	x 1
Byrne, Pte. (K.R.R.)	,,	31,	,,	13, L	B x 1
✓Brabant, Lieut. (I.L.H.)	Nov.	6,	,,	28, R	x 2
Butterworth, J., Pte. (1st Man.)	,,	13,	,,	16, L	B x 3
Brocket, Pte. (Devons)	,,	21,	,,	6, L	R x 3
Borrett, A. H.	Dec.	11,	,,	24, R	R 1
Bowles, N. C. (baby)	,,	11,	,,	24, R	W 2
Beard, R. B.	,,	11,	,,	8, L	C x 1
Broomhead, R. B.	,,	12,	,,	9, L	C x 1
Bowles, Sam. Victor	,,	13,	,,	24, R	W 2
Buxton, W. (Carbineers)	,,	18,	,,	31, R	x 3
Baylis, Pte. (Glo'sters)	,,	22,	,,	18, R	B x 1
Bailey, A., Bombardier (R.A.)	,,	23,	,,	8, L	B x 2
Black, James, Transport	,,	31,	,,	11, L	C x 1
					(See Webb)
Bartley, Pte., (1st Manch.)	Jan.	7,	1900	21, L	C x 1
Boon, Pte., (19th Hussars)	,,	8,	,,	15, L	C x 1
Borrett, J. T.	,,	20,	,,	24, R	W 22
Borrett, E, L.	Feb.	6,	,,	28, R	R 2
Blaker, Pte. (Rifle Brigade)	,,	9,	,,	7, L	C x 3
` Bryden, Chas. (Gordons)	,,	21,	,,	11, L	B x 3

C.

Name.	Date Buried.			No. of Grave.	Section.
Campbell, Lieut. (Gordons)	Oct.	23,	1899	11, R	x 2
Cunningham, J. (Volunteer)	,,	24,	,,	1, L	B x 1
Colville, A. W.	,,	25,	,,	4, L	B x 1
Chisholm, Col. Scott (I.L.H.)	,,	25,	,,	32, R	x 2
Couzens, Pte. (Glo'sters)	,,	25,	,,	6, L	B x 1

Burials—*continued.*

Name.	Date Buried.	No. of Grave.	Section.
Carr, E., Corpl. (Glo'sters)	Oct. 27, 1899	7	B x 1
Cleaver, W. (Carbineers)	,, 28, ,,	1, L	B x 1
Cooper, Shoeing Smith (19th Hussars)	,, 31, ,,	11, L	B x 3
Charlesworth, Pte. (K.R.R.)	,, 31, ,,	9, L	B x 1
Coward, Pte. (Glo'sters)	Nov. 1, ,,	15, L	B x 3
Crickmore, Jas. R.	Dec. 2, ,,	5, L	B x 2
Clacey, C. J.	,, 8, ,,	21, L	B x 3
Claridge, Corpl.	,, 8, ,,	28, R	x 3
Campbell, Agnes	,, 22, ,,	16, R	R 1
Clydesdale, T. R.	Jan. 1, 1900	7, R	x 2
Carbutt, Mary C.	,, 5, ,,	15, L	B 1
Creathead, M. (I.L.H.)	,, 7, ,,	12, L	B x 2
Cunningham, Dick, Col. (Gordons)	,, 7, ,,	7, R	x 3
Chadwick, Thomas Charles, Trooper (I.L.H.)	,, 9, ,,	18, L	B x 2
Cotton, W. N. Stapleton, Lieut. (19th Hussars)	,, 30, ,,	19, R	x 3
Crouch, Wm., Pte. (18th Hussars)	,, 30, ,,	17, R	x 4
Carbutt, Evelyn Grace	Feb. 17, ,,	15, L	B 1
Curtis, Pte. R., 79086 (R.I.F.)	,, 21, ,,	6	C x 2
Cornell, Corpl. E. (R.A.)	,, 22, ,,	19, L	C x 2
Collumbell, Pte. (2nd K.R.R.)	,, 26, ,,	15, L	B x 2

D.

Name.	Date Buried.	No. of Grave.	Section.
Daleny, J. (Manch.)	Oct. 23, 1899	3, L	B x 1
Davies, W. (Glo'sters)	,, 27, ,,	5, L	B x 1
Dearlove (I.L.H.)	Nov. 4, ,,	20, L	B x 3
Donohoe, Pte. (1st R.I.F.)	,, 5, ,,	17, R	x 2
Duncanson, Thos.	,, 22, ,,	9, R	x 2
Downing, J. (I.L.H.)	Dec. 19, ,,	20, L	B x 2
Dalziel, Lieut. (Devons)	,, 27, ,,	23, R	x 2
Dennis, G. B., 2nd Lieut. (R.E.)	Jan. 7, 1900	20, R	R 1
Doig, Dora Margory	,, 11, ,,	11, L	H 3
Denard, Colour-Sergt. (Glo'sters)	,, 12, ,,	7, L	H x 2
Darlison, Wm., Pte. (2nd B.R.B.)	,, 25, ,,	6, L	A x 2
Davies, W., Pte. (Glo'sters)	Nov. 3, ,,	3	B x 3
Doveton, Major (I.L.H.)	Feb. 14, ,,	18, R	x 3
Donovan, J., Pte. (2nd K.R.R.)	Oct. 31, ,,	11, L	B x 1
Dix, Pte. R. (Leicesters)	Feb. 22, ,,	14, L	C x 2

E.

Name.	Date Buried.	No. of Grave.	Section.
Egerton. Lieut. (R.N.)	Nov. 4, 1899	30, R	x 2
Elliot, T. (Carbineers)	Dec. 18, ,,	29, R	x 3
Ennion, W.	Feb. 28 1900	21, R	x 5

Burials—*continued.*

F.

Name.	Date Buried.	No. of Grave.	Section.
Foster, Lieut. (K.R.R.)	Oct. 31, 1899	31, R	x 2
		(See Marsden)	
Frilker, Corpl. (Gordons)	Nov. 15, ,,	4, L	B x 3
Finnimore, A. P. O. (1st Class, H.M.S. Powerful)	,, 22, ,,	25, R	x 2
Ferguson, Lieut.	Dec. 12, ,,	24, R	x 3
Fuller, F. W. (R.E.)	,, 18, ,,	13, L	C x 1
Fox, F. (B.M.R.)	Jan. 7, 1900	9, L	A x 3
Field, H. N., Lieut. (Devons)	,, 7, ,,	21, R	x 2
		(See Salter)	
Foreman, C., Pte. (Devons)	,, 7, ,,	19, L	C x 1
Forbes, Bella	,, 15, ,,	9, R	x 3
Forbes, C.	Feb. 3, ,,	10, R	x 3
Fielding, James	,, 7, ,,	12, L	C x 2
Fowlds, W.	,, 9, ,,		
Fraser, T., Driver (R.A.)	,, 24, ,,	19, R	x 4

G.

Name.	Date Buried.	No. of Grave.	Section.
Gray, E. W., Major (R.A.M.)	Oct. 31, 1899	15, R	x 2
Garner, Sergt.-Major (13th F.B.R.A.)	Nov 1, ,,	30, R	x 1
Goddard, Gunner (R.A.)	,, 19, ,,	19, L	B x 1
Geraghty, Pte.	Jan. 5, 1900	23, R	x 3
Gold, J. M. (B.M.R.)	,, 7, ,,	6, L	B x 2
Gradwell, S. W.	,, 21, ,,	1, R	R 1
Gore, H., Pte. (Glo'sters)	,, 22, ,,	20, L	B x 1

H.

Name.	Date Buried.	No. of Grave.	Section.
Heath, P. (Manch.)	Oct. 24, 1899	10, L	B x 1
Hargreaves, Pte. (K.R.R.)	,, 31, ,,	9, L	B x 1
Haslum, Pte. (Glo'sters)	Nov. 1, ,,	15, L	B x 3
Hibberd, Louis (R.E.)	Dec. 11, ,,	8, L	B x 3
Harries, John (2nd R. Brigade)	,, 12, ,,	4, L	G x 1
Homer, Drum (Glo'sters)	,, 22, ,,	16, R	B x 1
Hulley, P. R. (B.M.R.)	Jan. 7, 1900	9, L	B x 2
Hirrop, Silas (N.M.R.)	,, 9, ,,	27, R	R 1
Haley, Gunner (10th M.B.R.G.A.)	Feb. 4, ,,	12, L	C x 2
Humphrey, Pte. (Devons)	,, 8, ,,	4, L	B x 2
Hill, Pte. A. (2nd K.R.R.)	,, 27, ,,	11, L	A x 3

J.

Name.	Date Buried.	No. of Grave.	Section.
James, Gunner (R.A.)	Oct. 31, 1899	7, L	B x 3
Jefficote, Pte. (K.R.R.)	,, 31, ,,	9, L	B x 3
		(See Power)	

Burials—continued.

Name.	Date Buried.	No. of Grave.	Section.
Jackson, Bandsman (Manch.)	Nov. 10, 1899	8, L	A x 3
Jones, Digby, R.J.T. (R.E.)	Jan. 7, 1900	17, R	R 1
Johns, Geo. (H.M.S. Powerful)	,, 19, ,,	25, R	x 3

K.

Kelly, Pte.	Oct. 24, 1899	24, R	x 1
Knapp, Capt. S. C. (I.L.H.)	Nov. 4, ,,	29, R	x 2
Keech, Pte. C. (Rifle Brigade)	,, 14, ,,	14, L	B x 3
Kelly, Pte (Liverpools)	Jan. 24, 1900	18, L	C x 1
Kelly, H., Pte. (2nd K.R.R.)	,, 31, ,,	11, L	B x 1

L.

Leeson, Sergt. (2679)	Nov. 3, 1899	16, R	x 2
Lease (R.R.)	Dec. 14, ,,	23, R	W 2
Leighton, J. C. (Glo'sters)	,, 20, ,,	16, R	B x 1
Lawson, B. (B.M.R.)	Jan. 7, 1900	3, L	B x 2
Lafone, W. B., Capt. (Devons)	,, 7, ,,	22, R	x 2
Ledingham, Trooper (I.L.H.)	Feb. 21, ,,	16, L	B x 2

M.

Morgan, Bombardier (R.A.)	Oct. 31, 1899	5, L	B x 3
Myers, Major (K.R.R.)	,, 31, ,,	31, R	x 1
Marsden, Lieut. (K.R.R.)	,, 31, ,,	31, R	x 2
Mapstone, Sergt. (N.C.)	Nov. 5, ,,	15, L	B x 1
Mason, Math. (Leicesters)	,, 16, ,,	14, L	B x 1
Midwood, Driver (R.A.)	Dec. 16, ,,	10, L	C x 1
Miller, M. B. (Carbineers)	,, 18, ,,	33, R	x 3
Mocatt, Corpl. (I.L.H.)	Jan. 7, 1900	7, L	A x 1
Moir, Pte. (Gordons)	,, 7, ,,	30, R	x 3
Mitchell, Robt. (Journalist)	,, 12, ,,	27, R	1 1
Mackenson, Pte. (18th Hussars)	,, 22, ,,	15, L	C x 2
Mander, Sapper (R.E.)	Feb. 1, ,,	0, L	C x 2
McCabe, Pte. (Gordons)	Oct. 23, 1899	21, R	x 1
McNee, F. S., Sergt.	,, 25, ,,	8, L	B x 1
McDonald, Lieut. (R.A.)	,, 31, ,,	13, R	x 2
McCabe, F., Bandsman (Manch.)	Nov. 10, ,,	8, L	A x 3
McHarley, Pte.	Dec. 8, ,,	26, R	x 3
Mead, Mian James	Feb. 24, 1900	1, R	x 3
McCough, T., Pte. (2nd K.R.R.) 8193	,, 28, ,,	15, R	x 4

N.

Nichol, R. G.	Dec. 10, 1899	21, L	B x 2
Nalton	,, 22, ,,	23, R	R 1
Nichol, W. (Glo'sters)	,, 22, ,,	18, R	B x 1
Neilson, Pte. (B.M.R.)	Oct. 26, ,,	27, R	x 1
Newman, Chas.	Feb. 20, 1900	18, R	R 2

Burials—continued.

O.

Name.	Date Buried.	No. of Grave.	Section.
Oxenham, Corpl. (Glo'sters)	Dec. 22, 1899	20, R	B x 1
Obrien, Nurse Eleanor	,, 29, ,,	22, R	R 1

P.

Name.	Date Buried.	No. of Grave.	Section.
Patrick, Pte. (Leicesters)	Oct. 31, 1899	13, L	B x 3
Power, Trooper (I.L.H.)	,, 31, ,,	9, L	B x 3
Page, Pte. (Dragoons)	Nov. 4, ,,	5, L	A x 3
Pouzer, G., Pte. (1st Manch.)	,, 5, ,,	12, L	B x 3
Paterson (R.B.)	Dec. 11, ,,	6, L	C x 1
Prowitt, R. (19th Hussars)	,, 23, ,,	11, L	C x 1
Preece, Arthur	,, 30, ,,	2, R	x 2
Patmore, Lieut. (I.L.H.)	Jan. 7, 1900	21, L	B x 1
Pidgeon, G. (Devons)	,, 7, ,,	17, L	C x 1
Parkinson, Reuben, Pte. (5th Dragoon Guards)	,, 11, ,,	10, L	B x 2
Payne, Geo. (H.M.S. Powerful)	,, 22, ,,	21, R	x 4
Picket, J., Pte. (Glo'sters)	,, 25, ,,	6	B x
Pinkney, G. R.	Feb. 17, ,,	2, R	V 1

R.

Name.	Date Buried.	No. of Grave.	Section.
Rummeling, J. (Hollander from Pretoria)	Oct. 27, 1899	2, L	A x 3
Robertsons, H. C. (Leicesters)	,, 31, ,,	13, L	B x 3
Robinson, L. C. (Glo'sters)	Dec. 22, ,,	13, L	B x 2
Rich, T. B.	,, 31, ,,	34, R	x 3
Riley, Rich. (infant)	Jan. 1, 1900	21, R	R 1
Rodgers, F. (I.L.H.)	,, 7, ,,	14, L	B x 2
Rees, Wm. (5th Dragoon Guards)	,, 11, ,,	5, L	A x 2
Ridings, W. (2nd K.R.R.)	,, 14, ,,	17, L	B x 2

S.

Name.	Date Buried.	No. of Grave.	Section.
Sparks, W. L., Sergt. (Glo'sters)	Oct. 17, 1899	20	x 1
Stone, H.	,, 27, ,,	2, L	B x 1
Setlbrid, Pte. (R.R)	Nov. 12, ,,	27, R	x 2
Schranin, Geo. (M.M.R.)	,, 15, ,,	1, L	B x 2
Stark, Dr. A. C.	,, 19, ,,	26, R	x 2
Stewart (infant)	Dec. 22, ,,	22, R	W 2
Strachan, A. (N.G.R.)	Jan. 8, 1900	8, R	x 3
Seager, W., Pte. (Devons)	,, 9, ,,	4, L	A x 2
Stephens, A., Pte. (Glo'sters)	,, 9, ,,	19, R	x 2
Steevens, G. W. (Journalist)	,, 15, ,,	28, R	R 1
Stewart, H. (Gordons)	,, 27, ,,	22, R	x 1
Shaw, W. (Carbineers)	,, 27, ,,	19, R	R 2
Steadman, J. W., Corpl. (R.E.)	,, 29, ,,	2, L	C x 2
Smith, Gunner (R.A.)	,, 31, ,,	7, L	B x 3

Burials—continued.

Name.	Date Buried.	No. of Grave.	Section.
Stubbs, Driver (R.A.)	Jan. 31, 1900	5, L	B x 3
Saunders, Pte. (K.R.R.)	,, 31, ,,	13, L	B x 1
Smith, C. (Carbineers)	Dec. 18, 1899	27, R	x 3
Stewart (infant)	,, 27, ,,	22, R	W 2
			(See former)
Salter, A., Pte. (Devon)	Jan. 7, 1900	19, L	C x 1
Simmons, Sapper (R.E.)	,, 7, ,,	26, R	R 1
Stafford, Pte. (Manch.)	,, 20, ,,	21, R	x 3
Sharp, Cpl. (Manch.)	Feb. 8, ,,	13, L	A x 3
Stanger, Orderly (A.S.C.)	,, 8, ,,	10, L	A x 3
Southern, Pte.	,, 15, ,,	21, L	C x 2
Sears, Pte. E. (Leicesters)	,, 27, ,,	15, L	A x 3

T.

Name.	Date Buried.	No. of Grave.	Section.
Taunton, Major C. E. (Carbineers)	Nov. 4, 1899	18, L	B x 3
Todd, C. V. (N.G.R.)	Jan. 1, 1900	32, R	x 3

V.

Name.	Date Buried.	No. of Grave.	Section.
Venn, S. (Glo'sters)	Oct. 31, 1899	9	B x 3

W.

Name.	Date Buried.	No. of Grave.	Section.
Will, Pte. (Gordons)	Oct. 23, 1899	32, R	x 1
Willford, Col. (1st Glo'sters)	,, 25, ,,	12, R	x 2
Walker, Major (R.A.M.C.)	Jan. 5, 1900	8, R	x 2
Wade, F. B.	Dec. 1, 1899	2, L	B x 2
Weeks, Pte. (R.B.)	,, 11, ,,	3, L	C x 1
White, C., Pte. (Glo'sters)	,, 22, ,,	13, R	B x 2
Webb (18th Hussars)	Jan. 7, 1900	21, L	C x 1
			(See Bartley)
Walker, E. E. M., Lieut.	,, 7, ,,	22, R	x 3
Wallnutt, Hilleir, Major (Gordons)	,, 7, ,,	4, L	A x 1
Wingate, Trooper (I.L.H.)	,, 8, ,,	12, L	C x 1
Webber, Mary Ann	,, 10, ,,	18, R	R 1
Woods, W., Pte. (Devons)	,, 12, ,,	20, L	C x 1
Wileman, Corpl. (I.R.R.)	,, 18, ,,	8, L	C x 2
Warsop, J., Pte. (Leicesters)	,, 29, ,,	7, L	C x 2
White, W. S., Corpl. (Glo'sters)	Nov. 3, ,,	3	B x 3
Wheeler, Dudley (H.M.S. Powerful)	Jan. 10, ,,	6, L	A x 1
Wilson, C., Pte. (2nd K.R.R.)	Oct. 31, ,,	11, L	B x 1
Whitehead, Pte. (1st Leicesters)	Feb. 21, ,,	17, L	C x 2
Walker, Capt. (Surgeon)	,, 24, ,,	16, R	x 3

Y.

Name.	Date Buried.	No. of Grave.	Section.
York, Pte. (2nd K.R.R.)	Jan. 18, 1900	10, L	C x 2

RATIONS.

Statement showing particulars and value of supplies issued to the besieged residents during the last month of the siege.

Article.	Quantity.	Rate.	Amount. £ s. d.
Bread	6914 lbs.	16/- per 100 lbs.	55 6 3
Biscuit	6176 lbs.	6d. per lb.	154 8 0
Meat Ox	9741¾ lbs.	80/- per 100 lbs.	389 13 5
Tea	161 1-10 lbs.	1/6 per lb.	12 2 5
Sugar	1495 3-16 lbs.	23/6 per 100 lbs.	17 11 4
Salt	40 12-16 lbs.	1d. per lb.	3 5
Pepper	1 1-16 lbs.	1/6 per lb.	1 7
Paraffin Oil	8 gallons	3/- per gallon	1 4 0
Matches	2 doz.	1/- per doz.	2 0
Coffee	56½ lbs.	1/6 per lb.	4 4 9
Mealie Meal	828¼ lbs.	27/6 per 200 lbs.	5 13 10
			£640 11 0

INTOMBI CAMP.

ON the fourth of November, Sir George White, recognising the danger that might happen by reason of the constant shelling of Ladysmith, applied to General Joubert for permission to allow the Townspeople to leave for the South. At this date the General had established his camp at the Umbulwana, and during the early part of the day he replied emphatically declining to accede to the request; he, however, offered no objection to the wounded, with the military doctors and necessary nurses, together with such inhabitants who had not taken up arms, being removed to an isolated spot at short distance from the town, the exact site to be practically selected by himself. There were certain conditions to this permission. It was a stipulation that the number of civilians should be communicated to General Joubert, and they, together with the wounded, would have to take up their new quarters by sundown the following day. This "considerate" condescension was made known to the populace by Mr. Farquhar, the Mayor, during the course of the afternoon. Names were at once enrolled; some being eager to get away, while others resolutely declined to leave the town under the conditions laid down by the Boer leader. In due course the Camp became formed, boundaries fixed, and "the wounded, with the medical men, the necessary nurses, and the enrolled residents," took their departure by train for the newly-created station, "Intombi," on the Natal Government Railway, some four miles in a southerly direction from Ladysmith. The Camp forming the neutral ground was situate under the shadow of the Umbulwana, with the line of railway running through it from the 185½ to the 187 mile post, a distance of 1½ miles; the space occupied, including the Military Camp alongside, was 2,000 acres, all, with the exception of Wiltshire's farm of 100 acres, forming a portion of Town Lands. It was bounded on the South by Intombi Spruit, on the East by Klip River, on the North by Fourie's Spruit, and on the West by Town Lands bush. Throughout the siege the Camp was maintained, and the greatest discipline exercised; none of the civilians were allowed to take their departure or return to Town. Rations, together with necessaries required, were daily supplied from Ladysmith, under the direction and at the instance of the Military Authorities. On the 1st of February, from statistics obtained, the civilian population consisted of 428 Europeans; Natives numbered 378; and Indians 656. The average number of sick civilians in Hospital from 11th November to 31st January was 10·07; Natives and Indians, 6·12. The ailments of the sick were confined to diarrhœa, dysentery, and fever; in all there were 9 cases of enteric fever. The mortality was remarkably small—only 2 Europeans succumbed to fever, and 11 dysentery and diarrhœa; among the coloured people, the deaths were equally few, and these were chiefly among the children.

[It was the intention of the compiler to give a full list of the names of all the occupants of the Camp, but through the fire at the Publisher's premises the manuscript has been destroyed, and it is now found impossible to replace it.]

Military and Municipal Notices.

CHRISTMAS TREE.

All European children in Ladysmith are invited by Colonel Dartnell, C.M.G., and Major K. Davis to attend a Christmas party and Christmas tree in Messrs. Walton and Tatham's Hall this evening at 7.30 till 9.30.

Ladysmith, 25th Dec., 1899.

UNEMPLOYED.

Volunteers to assist in nursing of the sick at Ndomba Hospital are urgently required. Men willing to assist are requested to apply to

D. G. GILES, A.R.M.

27th December, 1899.

MILK SUPPLY.

Notice is hereby given that the Military Authorities wish it made known that in consequence of the urgent demand for milk in the hospitals, all purveyors of same within the Borough must on and after the 29th day of December inst. make arrangements to hand the daily supplies over to Mr. P. Nicholson, who will attend at Messrs. Scott and Hyde's Kraal (behind Messrs. Sparks Bros.' store) to receive the same.

Milk should reach the appointed place punctually every morning at 5 o'clock, and again in the evening at 6 o'clock.

Persons found disposing of milk to private individuals after the date named will be liable to have their cows taken over by the authorities without further notice.

The authorities will pay for the milk to be supplied 1s. per quart, or 8d. per bottle, and in addition they will provide bran and crushed mealies for the purpose of feeding the cows. This notice applies to all owners of milch cows.

J. FARQUHAR,
Mayor.

28th December, 1899.

A SOUVENIR.

As soon as circumstances will permit it is intended to have all residents of Ladysmith during the prolonged siege photographed in a group. A register is now open, and bona-fide residents are requested to communicate their names to the Town Clerk.

J. FARQUHAR,
Mayor.

28th December, 1899.

RULES AND REGULATIONS FOR THE MANAGEMENT AND CONDUCT OF A TEMPORARY HOSPITAL ESTABLISHED AT LADYSMITH BY THE MUNICIPAL AUTHORITIES DURING THE TIME OF THE SIEGE.

1. The name, to distinguish it from the Military Hospital, is, "The Ladysmith Borough Hospital."

2. Its management shall be in the hands of a committee, consisting of two members of the Town Council, viz., the Mayor and the Deputy Mayor.

3. No patient shall be admitted unless upon the recommendation of a local medical practitioner, with the approval of the committee.

4. Each patient shall be permitted to be attended by his own medical adviser, to whom he shall be responsible for all

fees incurred. The management will provide nursing accommodation, medicine, and medical comforts, bedding, and the like, the maximum charge for this being £2 2s. per week, or any portion of a week. The management shall have the power to forego the fee should the patient be in stringent circumstances and unable to pay.

5. The wards may be visited on Wednesdays and Sundays between 3 and 4 p.m.

6. There shall be one certificated nurse in charge, who shall devote the whole of her time to the duties in connection with the hospital. She shall report at least weekly to the management.

7. Should any assistant nurses be found necessary, they shall be appointed by the management, but nevertheless they shall be under the full control of the head nurse in charge.

8. No patient shall be discharged unless under the certificate of his medical adviser, which must at once be submitted to the management.

9. Requisitions for goods required shall be forwarded as often as needs be to the Town Clerk for the approval and signature of the committee.

10. The head nurse shall keep a register of patients admitted, giving full particulars of name, place of abode, and occupation, date of admission, discharge, or death, and all full particulars.

December, 1899.

RAILWAY TICKETS.

Copy of Letter from Town Clerk to Colonel Ward, A.A.G. (B.), Natal Field Force :—

18th December, 1899.—I am directed to write you with regard to certain resolutions adopted at a meeting of the Town Council held this morning. It was resolved to suggest that all Ladysmith and district residents now in Durban and elsewhere be permitted to return over the N.G.R. to their homes free of charge, and that the application for this purpose be made through Lieut.-General White, G.O.C., and also that priority be given over all other travellers.

"That all bona-fide besieged residents of Ladysmith and district be permitted the advantage of a free return ticket within the Colony over the N.G.R., available for fourteen days, this to be a forcible suggestion to the G.O.C., and that public intimation be duly advertised."

Copy of Letter in reply from Colonel Ward to Town Clerk :—

20th December, 1899.—I am directed by the G.O. Commanding the Natal Field Force to acknowledge receipt of your letter of the 18th inst., forwarding a copy of a resolution adopted at a meeting of Town Council of Ladysmith, held on the same day. I am directed by Sir George White to inform you that when communication by railway is re-opened he will forward the application to the officials of the N.G.R., in whose hands the granting of permission to travel over their lines free of charge will lie.

By order,

G. W. LINES,

January 4th, 1900. Town Clerk.

CONCERT.

A concert, to be held on the Volunteer Parade Ground, Ladysmith, will be given by the Warrant Officers and Non-Commissioned Officers and men of the combined Volunteer Corps on Wednesday, 3rd January, 1900, at 7.30 p.m.

Patron, Col. Royston, Commanding Volunteers; Chairman, R.-S.-M., Bowen, N.C. Committee : Messrs. Lord and Adrian, N.N.V.; Duff and Molyneux, N.C. ; Carmont and Turner, N.M.R ; McClellan and Alexander, B.M.R.; Flood and

Goodwin, Volunteer Signal Corps; Stage Manager, R.-M.-S. Parry, N.M.R.; Secretary, Sergt. Britten, B.M.R.

All the inhabitants of Ladysmith and members of the Garrison are cordially invited.

3rd January, 1900.

COPY OF ADDRESSES PRESENTED BY LADYSMITH CORPORATION.

To the Right Hon. Sir Redvers Henry Buller, P.C., G.C.B. K.C.M.G., V.C.

Sir,—We, the Mayor and Members of the Town Council of the Borough of Ladysmith, Natal, and as such representing the inhabitants of the said Borough, beg most respectfully to welcome with great joy the arrival of yourself and your gallant soldiers, and to express to you our most sincere and heartfelt appreciation of your noble and courageous efforts in the relief of this long-beleaguered Borough.

As members of the great British Empire, as loyal subjects of Her Most Gracious Majesty the Queen, and as Colonists of Natal, we beg respectfully to tender to you our most hearty thanks, realising as we do the magnitude and difficulty of the work accomplished.

At the same time our sympathies are great for the heavy losses among the brave troops that have occurred in your successful efforts to relieve us.

Given under our common seal, at Ladysmith, Natal, this 4th day of March, 1900.

To Lieut.-General Sir George S. White, V.C., G.C.B., G.C.S.I., G.C.I.E., Commanding the Natal Field Force.

Sir,—We, the Mayor and Members of the Town Council of the Borough of Ladysmith, Natal, and as such representing the inhabitants of the said Borough, beg to offer you our hearty congratulations and express gratitude for the very able manner in which you have organised the defence of this town during the prolonged siege of 120 days.

We fully recognise the difficulties and dangers which you have had to encounter in defending such an extended area, and that your efforts have been successful is shown by the signal manner in which the gallant troops under your command have resisted the repeated attacks of the Boer forces.

We trust that you may long be spared to continue your illustrious services to your Queen, and in the welfare of your country.

Given under our common seal, at Ladysmith, Natal, this 6th day of March, 1900.

SPOONS FOR HOSPITAL.

Spoons (tea and dessert size) are required for use in hospitals. Anyone having any to dispose of for that purpose, by gift or sale, is requested to communicate with the undersigned.

W. CLARE SAVILE, Major, R.A.,
Senior Ordnance Officer.

10th January, 1900.

INSTRUCTIONS FOR THE DISTRIBUTION OF FOOD TO THE CIVILIAN POPULATION OF LADYSMITH.

1. The Town Clerk will provide a certified list, stating the names of the individual, or, if a family, the number of persons in each (specifying children under 10 years of age), desirous of and recommended for rations.

2. An issuing depôt to be established at the Market House, with service counters and aisles railed off with wire, so as to admit single individuals to approach serving counters.

3. Issues will be made between the hours of 5 p.m. and 7 p.m. daily. Four issues will be detailed—one for groceries, one bread, one meat, and one for milk; also, a manager to be in charge of the supply establishment.

4. The following will be the procedure adopted when drawing rations :—On arrival at the Market Square, each person on being identified by an official to be deputed by the Mayor will receive from the office in the Market House a check for each description of supplies required, *i.e.*, one for meat, one bread, etc. The number of individuals entered on the check will be taken from the list rendered by the Town Clerk.

5. Two clerks will be provided, who will enter the amount of supplies on the checks, signing them before handing them to the individuals drawing the food. The checks will be filed by the issuers at once when making the issue, and before commencing to serve the next applicant.

6. The police will keep order, and see that only one person approaches the issuer at a time. They will remove any person making an obstruction, reporting the name of the offenders to the Deputy Assistant Adjutant General, Advanced Depôt, for such steps as he may consider necessary.

7. Notice boards will be placed to designate the office, etc.

RATIONS FOR CIVILIANS.

Preserved meat ½ lb., or fresh meat ¾ lb.; biscuits ½ lb., or bread 1 lb.; tea 1-6 oz.; sugar 1½ ozs.; salt ½ oz.

Note.—Half rations will be issued to children under 10 years of age.

---

8. Similar arrangements will be made for the issue of food to Indians and Kafirs. The distribution will be made at the Railway Station between 1.30 and 2.30, from the verandah of the new goods shed. The daily ration will be :

Indian Natives.—Atta 4 ozs., rice 3 ozs., mealie meal 9 ozs., salt ½ oz., goor 1¼ ozs., amchur ¼ oz. For those who eat meat, 8 ozs. twice weekly, atta and rice being withheld on these days.

Natives of South Africa.—Fresh meat 1 lb, mealie meal ¾lb., salt ½ oz.

The distribution both to civilians and natives will be under the supervision of Capt. Thompson, A.C.G.

All employers of labour will draw daily for the total number of their employees. Individual issues will not be made.

The list of those entitled to receive rations will be certified by the Town Clerk in a similar manner to that of the white population.

By order,

E. W. D. WARD,
Colonel,
A.A.G., Natal Field Force.

Ladysmith, January, 1900.

PAYMENT OF ACCOUNTS.

Contractors and others to whom money is due for oxen, stores, transport, etc., are requested to attend at the Field Pay Office, Advance Supply Depôt, Poort Road, between the hours of 9 a.m. and 5 p.m.

It is most essential that early application should be made, so that no delay may ensue.

By order,

A. HUNTER,
Major-General,
Chief of the Staff, Natal Field Force.

Ladysmith, 13th January, 1900.

TRAFFIC REGULATIONS.

Natal Field Force Order No. 466, dated 19th January, 1900.

With a view to obviating the blocks of traffic which frequently occur, the following rules are published for information, and will be strictly adhered to:—

Notices

1. (a) All vehicles are to be driven on the left of the road.

(b) One vehicle overtaking another to pass it on the right.

2. When passing along the Poort Road all vehicles proceeding in the same direction must keep their places, and not attempt to pass each other.

3. Whenever traffic is heavy, empty vehicles returning to the Railway Station, or other portions of Ladysmith, from above the Poort Road, are to proceed by Junction Hill, and not by the Poort Road. The Traffic Manager or one of his assistants will be stationed at the upper end of the Poort Road to direct the traffic.

4. Wagons which do not lock under are not to attempt to turn round on a road, but must choose the nearest suitably broad place off the road.

5. The number of horses or mules abreast when taken to water is not to exceed three.

6. Unless military exigencies render it necessary, a faster pace than a walk is strictly forbidden on the road running parallel to the river between the Iron Bridge and the Poort Road.

7. After dusk mules are to be led, and not driven.

8. Transport Officers are responsible that their conductors are in possession of a copy of these rules, and that they thoroughly explain to their drivers and leaders the purport thereof.

9. Soldiers, conductors, and drivers must strictly carry out any orders given them by the Traffic Director or his assistants.

10. Mr. Beresford Turner has been appointed Director of Traffic, Ladysmith, and Commanding Officers will issue instructions to conductors and white and native subordinates that they are to comply implicitly with instructions.

By order,

A. HUNTER,
Major-General,
Chief of the Staff, Natal Field Force.

Notices.

SALE OF WHISKEY.

To be sold by public auction at Scott and Hyde's Office on Thursday, 25th January, 1900, at 5 o'clock in the evening, one case Scotch whiskey (upset price £100), for the benefit of the widow of an officer who was killed in action.

SCOTT AND HYDE,
Auctioneers.

January 24th, 1900.

RAFFLE OF WHISKEY.

Colonel W. G. Knox will raffle on Tuesday, January 30th, 1900, at 5 o'clock, for the benefit of the widow of an officer killed in action, one dozen of Scotch whiskey. First prize, 6 bottles; 2nd prize, 4 bottles; 3rd prize, 2 bottles. Tickets, £1 each. Applications for tickets, accompanied by remittance, to be sent to Major H. B. Riddell, D.A A.G., Sec., A. Defence.

Note.—No raffle unless 100 tickets are subscribed for.

POSTAL NOTICE.

Ladysmith, 6th Feb., 1900.
Scheme for Garrison Postal Service—

A postal system will be organised in the Garrison for the receipt and delivery of official correspondence and letters not of a very urgent nature, such as returns, daily statements, etc., and letters not requiring an immediate answer. Private correspondence may also be sent by post.

For this purpose Ladysmith will be divided into nine districts.

1. Each district will have a letter box in as central a position as possible, and a bicycle orderly will be attached to each district. The orderlies will clear the boxes in their districts at stated times, and bring them to the General Post Office (next

to the Field Paymaster). The letters will then be sorted into districts and given to the orderlies of the various districts, who will then deliver them to the addresses, and return to the post office of their district to await the next clearance.

2. Small parcels, not exceeding 2 ozs., may be sent by post. Money or valuables if sent will be taken at the sender's risk.

3. The times of clearance and delivery of letter boxes will be approximately as under:—Clearance: 6 a.m., 10 a.m., 2 p.m., 4.30 p.m. Delivery: 8 a.m., 12 noon, 4 p.m., 6 p.m.

4. Staff Officers, Detached Officers, Medical Officers, and other Officers who do not live with their units, are requested to send their addresses to the Postmaster-General for registration. They should state clearly where their quarters are situated so as to facilitate the delivery of letters.

5. Letters will only be delivered to such civilians as are employed by the Imperial Government. Press correspondents may use the post if they have previously notified their addresses to the P.M.G.

6. The senders of letters are particularly requested to put the letters denoting the district in which the addressee is to be found. Thus: S.W., N.W., etc.

7. All enquiries should be addressed to the P.M.G., General Post Office, Central District.

By order,

A. HUNTER,
Chief of the Staff, Natal Field Force.

EGGS FOR HOSPITAL.

Ladysmith, 12th February, 1900.

In a letter from Colonel Ward, A.A.G., Natal Field Force, he refers to the great number of soldiers who are now suffering from enteric fever and other diseases of a similar character, and Colonel Exham, the Principal Medical Officer, informs him that if 200 eggs could be procured a day the greatest benefit would ensue to these sick men; in fact, in the majority of cases, material assistance would be rendered towards a satisfactory recovery.

At the request of Lieut.-General Sir G. White, Colonel Ward has written me upon the subject, and it is suggested that, if only a certain number of the inhabitants would give a few eggs, the required number could be obtained.

I shall be pleased to know from you at the earliest date possible, whether you will kindly assist by giving a few daily; and upon hearing from you to that effect, I shall be pleased to receive and forward same in accordance with the wishes of the Military Authorities herein expressed.

J. FARQUHAR,
Mayor.

NIGHT SALES.

I certify that the following are the correct and highest prices realised at my sales by public auction during the siege:—
14 lbs. oatmeal, £2 19s. 6d.; condensed milk, per tin, 10s.; 1 lb. beef fat, 11s.; 1 lb. tin coffee, 17s.; 2 lbs. tin tongue, £1 6s.; 1 sucking pig, £1 17s.; eggs, per dozen, £2 8s.; fowls, each, 18s. 6d.; 4 small cucumbers, 15s. 6d.; green mealies, each, 3s. 8d.; small plate grapes, £1 5s.; 1 small plate apples, 12s. 6d.; 1 plate tomatoes, 18s.; 1 vegetable marrow, £1 8s.; 1 plate eschalots, 11s.; 1 plate potatoes, 19s.; 3 small bunches carrots, 9s.; 1 glass jelly, 18s.; 1 lb. bottle jam, £1 11s.; 1 lb. tin marmalade, £1 1s.; 1 doz. matches, 13s. 6d.; 1 packet cigarettes, £1 5s.; 50 cigars, £9 5s.; ¼ lb. cake "Fair Maid" tobacco, £2 5s.; ½ lb. cake "Fair Maid," £3 5s.; 1 lb. sailor's tobacco, £2 3s.; ¼ lb. tin "Capstan" Navy Cut tobacco, £3.

JOE DYSON, Auctioneer.
Ladysmith, Feb. 21st, 1900.

Notices.

Travelling without a Ticket.—At the Police Court to-day Alfred Smith was summoned for travelling on the N.G.R. without previously having paid his fare. The defendant expressed regret for his conduct and declared that he did not wish to defraud the Government; he was simply on his way to receive rations from the Corporation Store. He was discharged without a caution.

EGGS FOR THE SICK AND WOUNDED.

Notice is hereby given that by request of the General Officer Commanding, owners of fowls within the Borough must hand over all eggs to the Municipal Authorities for the use of the sick and wounded.

Upon intimation being given to the Town Clerk, at the office of Messrs. Walton and Tatham, arrangements will be made daily to collect and receive the same, or they can be forwarded to him direct at the office in question, between the hours of 9 a.m. and 1 p.m. (Sundays excepted).

Failing this notice being fully observed by 12 o'clock noon on Monday, the 26th inst., the Military Authorities intimate through the undersigned, that owners, with no exception, will be compelled to hand over their fowls for the purpose of supplying the eggs now so urgently required.

J. FARQUHAR,
Mayor.

24th February, 1900.

PERMISSION TO REMAIN IN THE BOROUGH.

Whilst a state of war lasts no non-resident will be allowed to remain in Ladysmith without special permission of the General Officer Commanding the Troops, or of the Officers deputed by him.

The Magistrate and District Police will give effect to this order at once.

All unauthorised persons will leave within 24 hours, on pain of being arrested.

Opportunities will be afforded for them to leave by railway.

(By order),
A. HUNTER,
Major-General,
Chief of Staff, Natal.

Ladysmith, 29th October, 1899.

THE NATAL BANK, LIMITED, LADYSMITH.

The premises of the above Bank having been taken over by the Military Authorities, all clients wishing to transact business are requested to communicate with the Manager, c/o Natal Bank, Durban, 31st October, 1899.

BOMBARDMENT DANGERS.

The G.O. Commanding can make no compulsory order. The dangers arising from the bombardment of the town are well known to all, and it is at the option of the remaining residents to leave or stay as they may think proper.

(By order),
A. HUNTER,
Major-General,
5th November, 1899. Chief of Staff, Natal.

RATIONS.

Supplies will be given out at Mr. Marsh's store, opposite the Town Hall, at 5.30 p.m. on Thursday, 9th November, and succeeding days.

(By order),
G. W. LINES,
Town Clerk.

PASS TO REMAIN.

In order to avoid unnecessary inconvenience to the civilian population of Ladysmith, the Lieut.-Gen. Commanding directs that all civilian inhabitants and natives, not wearing uniforms, shall be in possession of a pass signed by the Magistrate or by one of the Headquarters Staff.

After daylight on Sunday, the 12th November, all persons not in possession of such passes will be detained by the Police.

Printed forms of passes can be obtained from the Magistrate or the Headquarter Office.

By Order,

A. HUNTER, Major-Gen.
Chief of the Staff, Natal Field Force.

Ladysmith, November 11th, 1899.

FORM OF PASS.

The Bearer,
    Name ....
    Nationality ....
    Age ....
    Complexion...
    Height..
    Hair... ....
    Occupation ....
has permission to remain in Ladysmith.

For Chief of Staff, Natal Field Force.

Ladysmith, Nov., 1899.

SUGGESTED PERMISSION FOR NON-COMBATANTS TO LEAVE THE BOROUGH.

Sir George White has written to General Joubert to suggest that non-combatants—men, women, and children—be permitted to leave Ladysmith, and is awaiting his reply.

Notices.

Meanwhile, Sir George suggests that, if the town is bombarded, he thinks the safest place is near or beyond the Grand Stand on the Race Course, and that anybody proceeding there may go under a white flag to show they have no connection with the combatant forces of the garrison.

(Signed),

A. HUNTER,
Major-General.

4th November, 1899.

EXTRACT FROM THE TRANSLATION OF A LETTER DATED NOV. 4TH, 1899, FROM COMMANDANT-GENERAL JOUBERT TO SIR GEO. WHITE, LIEUT.-GENERAL COMMANDING THE BRITISH TROOPS, NATAL.

"Respecting your request that the townspeople may be allowed to leave for the South, this I cannot possibly agree to. The wounded, with their attendants and doctors, may, as requested by you, be taken to a chosen place; and I shall agree that the people of the town shall also be removed there.

"The number of the civilians must be communicated to me, and the removal of the wounded and civilians must be effected within 24 hours of the receipt of this, and the locality must be distinctly marked.

"I must further make it a condition that under the name of civilian there must not be sent out any who have taken up arms against the Republic."

True extract of letter received at Ladysmith on 4th November, 1899, at 12 noon.

A. HUNTER,
Major-General,
Chief of Staff, Natal.

WATER SUPPLY OF LADYSMITH.

Regulations for the Supply of Water to the Garrison and Civil Population of Ladysmith.

1. Water will be laid on from the old town source, which will deliver a supply to the town through the delivery pipes, with the exception of those belonging to houses in that portion which lies north of the Railway Station.

2. Water can be obtained from tanks (which have been placed in the lane at the foot of the Poort Road) by the troops and civilians, at the hours after mentioned. It will be necessary for civilians to bring vessels, casks, carts, or other means of storage. The troops will use the water-carts in their possession :—

   Military............... 6 a.m. to 8 a.m.
   Civil population ... 8 ,, 11 ,,
   Military............... 11 ,, 2 p.m.
   Civil population ... 2 p.m. to 4 ,,
   Military............... 4 ,, 7 ,,

3. There are, as at present reported, 8 wells in Ladysmith, viz. :—

   A—One in jail.
   B—Four east side Lyle Street (between Town Hall and river).
   C—One in upper end of Lyle Street.
   D—One in Railway Hotel.
   E—One in Mr. Linthorp's property.

The distribution of these wells will be as follows :—

   A—Civil officials and officials of Public Works Department.
   B—Military.
   C, D, and E—Civil population.

4. The wells at B will be guarded by the military, and their use will be made as follows :—

   A—5 a.m. to 8 a.m.—Headquarter Staff and troops north of Princess Street.

B—8 a.m. to 11 a.m.—Hospitals and those situated in the district between Princess Street and Albert Street.
C—11 a.m. to 2 p.m.—Troops north of Albert Street.
D—2 to 3.30 p.m.—Troops as at A.
E—3.30 to 5 p.m.—Troops as at B.
F—5 to 6.30 p.m.—Troops as at C.

5. The distribution to civil officials will be carried out under the supervision of Mr. Brooke, Public Works Department; that of the civil population under instructions to be issued by the Mayor.

The supply to troops will be carried out under the directions of an Officer of the Army Service Corps, who will arrange that each Corps is served in order of the arrival of its water-cart at the wells or tanks.

By order,
A. HUNTER,
Major-General,
Chief Staff Officer Natal Field Force.

November, 1899.

CAUTION REGARDING UNAUTHORISED PERSONS OBTAINING FOOD SUPPLIES.

It having come to the notice of the General Officer Commanding the Natal Field Force that certain unauthorised persons have requisitioned food supplies, including live cattle, for their own use, under the pretext that such food supplies were for consumption by Her Majesty's Forces, or of the civilians for whose nourishment the General Officer Commanding is at present providing, it is hereby notified that such proceedings by those unauthorized persons are illegal, and will be most severely punished. It is hereby directed that information which will lead to the arrest of any individuals guilty of this offence should at once be given to the Provost-Marshal or the Acting Magistrate.

The Officers authorized to make such requisitions on behalf of the General Commanding the Natal Field Force are :—

Notices.

Colonel E. W. D. WARD, C.B., Assistant Adjutant-General.
Lieutenant-Colonel J. STONEMAN, Deputy Assistant Adjutant-General.
Major E. R. O. LUDLOW, Deputy Assistant Adjutant-General.

Receipts, in detail, for all supplies obtained by Purchase or Requisition, are given by the above-named Officers, a Copy thereof being retained by the Vendors, and Bills for the payment of their value should be submitted by the latter in order that immediate settlement of the Claims may be made by the Paymaster to Her Majesty's Forces in Natal.

By Order,
A. HUNTER, Major-General.
Chief of the Staff, Natal Field Force.

Extracts from the Army Act published for the general information of the civilian inhabitants of Ladysmith :—

Section 4—Every person subject to Military Law who commits any of the following offences; that is to say—

(1) Shamefully abandons or delivers up any garrison, place, post, or guard, or uses any means to compel or induce any governor, commanding officer, or other person shamefully to abandon or deliver up any garrison, place, post, or guard, which it was the duty of such governor, officer, or person to defend; or

(2) Shamefully casts away his arms, ammunition, or tools in the presence of the enemy; or

(3) Treacherously holds correspondence with, or gives intelligence to the enemy, or treacherously or through cowardice sends a flag of truce to the enemy; or

(4) Assists the enemy with arms, ammunition, or supplies, or knowingly harbours or protects an enemy not being a prisoner; or

(5) Having been made a prisoner of war, voluntarily serves with or voluntarily aids the enemy; or

(6) Knowingly does, when on active service, any act calculated to imperil the success of Her Majesty's forces or any part thereof; or

(7) Misbehaves or induces others to misbehave before the enemy in such a manner as to show cowardice;

shall, on conviction by Court-Martial, be liable to suffer death or such less punishment as is in this Act mentioned.

Section 5—Every person subject to Military Law who on active service commits any of the following offences, that is to say—

(1) Without orders from his superior officer leaves the ranks in order to secure prisoners or horses, or on pretence of taking wounded men to the rear; or

(2) Without orders from his superior officer wilfully destroys or damages any property; or

(3) Is taken prisoner, by want of due precaution, or through disobedience to orders or wilful neglect of duty, or having been taken prisoner fails to rejoin Her Majesty's Service when able to rejoin the same; or

(4) Without due authority either holds correspondence with or gives intelligence to, or sends a flag of truce to the enemy; or

(5) By word of mouth or in writing, or by signals, or otherwise, spreads reports calculated to create unnecessary alarm or despondency; or

(6) In action, or previously to going into action, uses words calculated to create alarm or despondency; shall, on conviction by Court-Martial, be liable to suffer penal servitude, or such less punishment as is in this Act mentioned.

By Order,

A. HUNTER, Major-General,
Chief of the Staff, Natal Field Force.

Ladysmith, Nov. 30, 1899.

Notices.

ROYAL MILITARY TOURNAMENT.
Natal Field Force, Ladysmith.

By kind permission and under the patronage of Lieutenant-General Sir GEORGE S. WHITE, V.C., G.C.B., G.C.S.I., G.C.I.E, Commanding the Natal Field Force.

CHRISTMAS DAY, 1899, or NEW YEAR'S DAY, 1900.
(As circumstances may permit.)
Commencing at 1 p.m. on the Old Polo Ground, Tin Camp.

COMMITTEE.
PRESIDENT.
Lieut.-General Sir GEORGE S. WHITE, V.C., G.C.B., G.C.S.I., G.C.I.E.

CHAIRMAN.
Major-General Sir A. HUNTER, K.C.B., D.S.O.

Major-General I. F. BROCKLEHURST, M.V.O., Commanding Cavalry Brigade.
Colonel C. M. A. DOWNING, C.R.A.
Colonel DARTNELL, C.M.G., Commanding Natal Police.
Colonel I. S. M. HAMILTON, C.B., D.S O., Commanding 7th Brigade.
Major-General F. Howard, C.B., C.M.G., A.D.C., Commanding 8th Brigade.
Colonel W. G. KNOX, C.B., Commanding Divisional Troops.
Captain the Hon. HEDWORTH LAMBTON, R.N., Commanding Naval Brigade.
Colonel W. Royston, Commanding Volunteer Forces.

WORKING COMMITTEE.
One Officer from Head Quarter Staff, Naval Brigade, each Regiment Brigade Division, R.A., Battalion, and from R.E., A.S.C.

Names to be sent to Honorary Secretary by 6 p.m., on 24th December, 1899.

Colonel E. W. D. WARD, C.B., Hon. Sec.
Captain W. A. TILNEY, 17th Lancers, Hon. Treas.

Notices.

WATER.

The water from this hydrant is unfit for drinking purposes.
December 2, 1899.

MARKET.

Notice is hereby given that the Morning Market is for a time discontinued; the re-opening of the Railway will see its resuscitation.

(By order),
G. W. LINES,

December 10, 1899.   Market Master.

PRODUCE SALES.

To obviate the inconvenience caused by the Town Council discontinuing the Market, the undersigned will hold sales of produce every Saturday and Wednesday evenings until further notice, at 7 o'clock. Good mutton always on sale.

December 15, 1899.

SCOTT & HYDE.

"LIGHTS OUT."

Notice is hereby given that the G.O.C. has issued no order with regard to "lights out" at 8.30 p.m., as a restriction of this nature, Sir G. White thinks, would much inconvenience the inhabitants of the Borough.

By Order,
December 22, 1899.   Town Clerk.

TIME.

Notice is hereby given that a clock has been placed at the Post Office, which denotes the official time.

By Order,
TOWN CLERK.

4th January, 1900.

The Ladysmith Bombshell.

LONG TOM O' PEPWORTH'S HILL.

He doth not speak in parable,
   Or whisper soft and low,
So all the folk of Ladysmith
   His every accent know;
For he can bend the stiffest back,
   And mould the strongest will—
He's quite a little autocrat,
   Long Tom o' Pepworth's Hill.

We listen when he speaks in wrath
   We're braver when he cools;
Yet is he very kind to men,
   If somewhat rough on mules.
He brings us bounding out of bed
   When we would fain be still—
We grumble, but we all obey
   Long Tom o' Pepworth's Hill.

A breezy, bluff, intrusive sort,
   He visits everywhere;
Sometimes he seeks your cellar cool,
   Sometimes your easy chair;
Sometimes he enters by the roof,
   Sometimes the window-sill—
It's vain to say you're not at home
   To Tom o' Pepworth's Hill.

                D. M. D.

The Town Clock according to official time is correct.

LESSONS IN DUTCH.—Mr. Lotter begs to announce that he has opened a select class for instructions in Dutch. In consequence of the increasing number, he is now able to receive a few additional pupils. (No connection with the establishment opposite.)

There was a time at the Royal when you got eggs inside and shells outside. Now you don't.

BAGS OF SAND.—"Quantity" exchanged for used stamps.— Apply Craddock, P.O.

A SHOT FIRED ON MAJUBA.—Mr. Greenwood has just returned from Majuba. He ascended the mountain, and, when on the topmost ridge overlooking the Free State side, he heard the report of a rifle, and a second later the peculiar whirr of a bullet fired in the air. In the valley below he distinguished, through a powerful pair of glasses, a large number of horses, with several men guarding them, but he could not distinguish any man carrying a rifle. No further shot was fired, and whether the single shot was intended to scare the correspondent from the ridge of the mountain, or only as a joke, it is impossible to discover.

The climatic conditions continue unsettled; this morning is fair and dry. There are, however, ominous clouds over the Umbulwana.

Mr. Woodhouse, the ex-Mayor of P. M. B., is making an extended visit to Ladysmith; he is anxious to get away.

Applications are invited for the post of President of the new Transvaal Republic. White men with a V.C. preferred.

For Sale.—One hundred Sworn Affidavits by Transvaal Burghers, regarding the inhuman treatment they received at the hands of the " Verdomde Engelsche," by being compelled to wash daily.

Wanted a few Dutchmen to enter the Town of Ladysmith. A warm reception guaranteed.

For Sale.—A few descriptions of the fights by eminent London correspondents. To be sold at a sacrifice.

" Now we shan't be long," getting to Durban "after" we have captured Ladysmith, is a favourite song among the white Dutchmen on the Umbulwana.

Col. Rhodes has taken the residence of Captain D——y for remainder of the shooting season.

At the Police Court this morning an application was made to the sitting Magistrate for an Order to arrest General Joubert, on the charge of disturbing the public peace, after the hour of 11 p.m. on the 14th inst. The necessary Order was at once granted. Sergt. M——r assured His Worship that, under a flag of truce, he would immediately effect service. It is anticipated the offender will be severely dealt with. (The maximum fine is £5.)

By request the following information is published :

I, the undersigned, a British subject, on condition of being allowed to proceed to the neutral zone or area known as Tombahs Spruit, do now promise and undertake (swear when I get there) to give no information to the advance column, and to hold no communication whatever with the enemy, until being removed to Pretoria under escort. (This declaration can be made before a J.P. at the Laager.)

"Trogloditic Conchologist." What is it? One who dwells in a cave, and sallies forth at cease firing to collect shells.

Officer with eye-glass meeting an aged mule in the street: "Dear me, 'pon my word, this, surely, must be a Boah."

Tenders for the erection of a Bridge at the River, near Kings, are invited. Apply, the Hon. Capt. D——y, Pretoria.

General Joubert is spending a few days with our Senior Member at Rietfontein. He is particularly interested in Mr. Pepworth's fine breed of cattle, and has purchased from him several of his pedigree bulls.

Where did that last shell fall? Don't know, old man, I'm not seeking shells, but shelter.

Carter's little Liver Pills. Perfectly safe and harmless. Two sufficient.

For Sale, a large Water Tank; slightly damaged.—Apply next the Church.

Now published, second edition, "The Shelling of a Scotch House," by MacPubert.

Missing Friends and Relatives.—Anxious enquiries are made for the following: W. M. A——d, H. G——r, An——F, P. R. A——n, H. G. N. H——d; last seen near the bar at Durban.

Lost, a Pluck.—Finder will be suitably rewarded upon returning same to Excavation No. 401, River Bank.

Lost, a Kit (hairdressing); last seen in the vicinity of River Bank.—Whoever will restore the same to Central Murchison Street will be rewarded with the thanks of the entire community.

> Lost, Stolen, or Strayed,
> Some men from the Town Guard Brigade.
> When last they were seen they were near the canteen,
> Whence tracks for the White Camp they made.

A grand smoking concert was held last evening in the Mammoth Cave, on the bank of Klip River, when the following programme was presented:—

"I know a Bank"	Mr. Davenport.
"I was near it"	Kit Harburn.
"Down by the river-side I stray"	Mr. Willis.
"Far, far away"	Dr. J——n.
"Shall we gather at the river?"	Mr. Turner.
"Oh, come unto these yellow sands"	Dr. Rouilliard.
"I know what it is to be there"	Mr. Brandon.
"Oh, why did I leave my little back room!"	Mr. Swigeson.

N.B.—A select concert will be held in the smoke-room at the Royal this evening.

Surveys undertaken in any part of the Division.—Apply, G. F. T.; temporary office, the War Balloon.

A large selection of Spy-glasses.—Apply, Mr. Lotter, on the Balcony.

Entrance to the Club may be made from Lyle Street; always open.

𝕿𝖍𝖊 𝕷𝖆𝖉𝖞𝖘𝖒𝖎𝖙𝖍 𝕭𝖔𝖒𝖇𝖘𝖍𝖊𝖑𝖑.

Something new in Hats—Mr. W. Y. H——r.

That you can talk about Ladysmith in any part of the civilized world now without being asked, Where is it?

The legistature is about to pass an act to prevent lying by telegraph. What is to become of " special despatches "?

An unfortunate shoeless donkey straying in the yard of the Royal Hotel walked into Butler's blacksmith shop of his own accord, and was there shoed by Mr. Butler, who naturally supposed his master somewhere in attendance. As soon as he had his shoes, the donkey, acting on an understanding of the principle of commercial credit, walked off without paying, and has not since been heard from. (It is conjectured he has been commandeered.)

> Sweetly, sweetly came the moonlight,
>   Through the window calm and fair,
> Then I thought that Tom was ready
>   For to say his morning prayer.
> Quickly, fiercely rose the murmur,
>   Through the stillness pure and deep,
> And that prayer was heard around us—
>   Then I laid me down to sleep.

TO GET RID OF MOSQUITOES.—Mosquitoes prefer beef blood better than they do anything that flows in the veins of human kind. Just put a couple of pieces on plates near your bed at night, and you sleep untroubled by these pests. In the morning you will find them full and stupid, and the meat sucked as dry as an ordinary railway hotel customer. Fresh beef, well suited for the purpose, can be obtained at the ration shop—free to residents only.

Printed and Published at Ladysmith, Natal, 18 Nov., 1899.

STRANGE ACCIDENT.—A very singular accident, anatomically considered, occurred on Friday morning near the Post-office. Mr. Craddock, while attempting to sit upon the shaft of a Scotch-cart, fell in such a manner as to strike the larynx, or upper part of the wind-pipe, upon a projecting nail with such force as to break through the larynx, though the skin was not wounded; and although he did not at first seem much hurt, he looked extremely uncomfortable and the air came rushing out with fearful rapidity. There being no external opening, it passed into the cellular texture and was driven on under the skin, obliterating every natural feature of his countenance, closing his eyes, elevating the scalp, and then passing down, nearly surrounded the chest and upper abdominal integuments. Dr. Rouilliard was passing at the time, and the necessary relief being afforded, Mr. Craddock proceeded on his way with Mr. Lotter to breakfast.

Having lost so many kernels at Elands Laagte, the Boers are now actively engaged in throwing away the shells.

It is authentically reported that the Umbulwana is now occupied by two men and a boy only.

Please, sir, can you lend mother a few sheets of iron; she wants to make a cave in the back garden, and father is away at Intombi Spruit playing in a cricket match.

For Sale, a few specimens of Boer shells; guaranteed not to kill. Apply, The General.

£10 Reward to the first Boer who enters Ladysmith in any capacity other than bearer of a white flag or as prisoner of war.

Amid all the din of shot and shell may frequently be heard the dulcet tones of the Deputy-Mayor's cornet.

MALONEY.

    I was a rolling blade of the Irish Brigade
        Of Joubert's, and fond of orating ;
    I'm hungry for foight, shoore
    I'll kill 'em all right,
        I'm hungry for want of a bating.
    Lave a hoult on me head ;
    Let me at 'em, he said,
        Put me up on a horse or a pony ;
    An' I'm sthrong an' I'm tall-talk,
    I'll slaughter thim all—
        For there's no sich a man as Maloney !

    He was a bombadier gay of the gallant R.A.,
        And the pride of the force, and they know it ;
    Went out for a walk ; heard that orator talk ;
        His answer was simply, "'Ere, stow it ! "
    He slipped in a shell, and he rammed it home well ;
        It burst on a ridge bleak and stony—
    It grieves me to say when the smoke cleared away
        There was no such a man as Maloney !

The prospects for business in Ladysmith are now so discouraging that some of the storekeepers have made an appeal to their landlords for a reduction in rents.

The latest information is to the effect that the Boer fleet, composed of the captured armoured train on two punts, is sailing up the Tugela *en route* for Gilestown, to intercept any flank movement on the part of the British troops.

Messrs. Surgeson and Brandon wish it noted that in consequence of official engagements they were unable to take part in the concert referred to in our last issue.

The Ladysmith Bombshell.

Someone was enquiring on Friday about the rainfall. He was told that statistics of the shell fire only were now taken.

Cool Cheek.—Natal Carbineer (talking of Mrs. ———, in whose yard he is quartered): "Oh, that lady! Why, she belongs to our camp."

The Borough of Ladysmith was shelled on November 2nd, 1899.

    All within the leaguered Borough,
      Calm and peaceful as of yore,
    Sat the people silently waiting
      The dread cannons' awful roar.

    Overhead the sun was shining,
      All serene the landscape lay,
    Waiting for the great disturbance,
      All expected on that day.

    Then broke forth a voice of thunder,
      With the shock the air was rent;
    Overhead there came a something,
      Instant every head was bent.

    Part a whistle, part a howling,
      Part a scream, and part a yell;
    Then a shock—a noise of bursting—
      'Twas the "murmur of the shell."

Natal Carbineer, as a shell flies in the vicinity of his tent, "Bother these fellows, they're getting careless with their shooting! If they don't look out, they'll be hurting somebody."

Gordon Highlander (whose pannikin has just been filled with sand by the bursting of a shell not three yards away): "D—— it all; that's the third time they've spoilt my tea."

Say, old man, if it takes Joubert and 23,579 Boers 23 days and three midnight hours to kill four white men and two Kaffirs, at what hour on what date will the last of the population of Ladysmith be exterminated?

Councillor Jones is daily taking a couple of doses of Mother Seigel's Soothing Syrup.

Information is requested regarding the name of the townsman who alleged a few days ago that the Geneva Convention was drawn up for the protection of residents of Funkdorp.

The other day when the Boers attacked Colenso, the women obtained permission from Piet to leave the little village carrying with them whatever they deemed most valuable. What was the surprise of the besiegers when they sallied forth, each carrying her husband on her back!—but Piet kept his word.

TO GENERAL SLIM PIET.

Hail, mighty Oom! Jew Beer,
   Proud leader of a dirty crew
Who shell at night, instead of fight,
   As savage Bourbon Tartars do.

Your deeds of valour, at the sound
   The nations well may quake:
The sick and wounded down you strike,
   The Church and Town Hall break.

The native folk you blandly strip
   Of cattle, clothes, and money,
And thus you prove you're closely bred
   To sow, and wolf, or monkey.

> Oh, slippery one, at last you've hit
>   The biggest marks in town;
> Days twenty-four you've done your best
>   To shell the Red Cross down.
>
> But still it waves, and at its back
>   Stands honour, brave and true;
> Our warrior lads but wait the word
>   To meet, and shave, and square with you.

To be raffled.—The last bottle of old Gaelic. 25 members a 1s. each. Optional on winner's part to stand drinks. Mr. Murray, the Club.

Messrs. Glover, Fraser, Cochran, and Shearer, formerly of Ladysmith, have attached themselves to the Durban Town Guard, and are doing good service.

A few of the Burgesses have clubbed their funds with the view of purchasing "Silent Susan," to be used on public occasion for the purpose of dispersing Scottish gatherings, and as occasion may require.

One of our young ladies, a refugee from Dundee, is so refined in her language, that she never uses the word "blackguard," but substitutes "African Sentinel."

A large collection of white flags to be disposed of in the Boer lines; these flags have been repeatedly used, but are good as new.

PROPOSED PRESENTATION TO MR. COUNCILLOR JONES.

A proposal has now taken shape for making some presentation to Mr. Jones, the worthy host of the Royal, on his retiring (of course temporarily) from the active pursuits of business, and in recognition of the excellent services he has rendered to the legion of war correspondents and the public in general during the siege of Ladysmith. At a largely-attended meeting held at the Royal last evening, Mr. Melton Prior in the chair, it was unanimously agreed to form a committee to consider what steps should be taken to further the recognition of Mr. Jones's services during the time mentioned. Mr. Rena kindly agreed to act as hon. sec. Mr. Jones wishes it known that upon the occasion of his forty-seventh birthday, which event takes place on the 30th inst., the hotel will be reopened for a short time in the evening. Any British friend will receive a warm welcome, and the auspicious occasion will be marked by the distribution of some dozen cases of champagne, which, after a good deal of adroitness, has been specially saved for the purpose. Mr. Jones has not gone to Intombi's Spruit, but simply resting a few days at his rural retreat.

In times of siege the lawyers cease from troubling; their clients need a rest.

Mr. Surgeson wishes it made known that extensive alterations have recently been made to the Oval; he is now actively engaged in preparing the programme for the Christmas fixture and anxious to receive entries. Colonel K——x on his whippet is a competitor in the big event.

Lost, my Adopted Child, named Transvaal Independence; when last seen was in the company of her sister, named Free State, following a German band. Anyone finding and returning the same to my new residence, St. Helena, will be rewarded with a confiscated gold mine.—J. S. P. Kruger.

Pretoria, November 19th, 1899.—From Joubert to Kruger. —Having heard that England has annexed the moon, last n ght opened a vigorous fire on it. Eventually moon retired behind a cloud. Casualties on our side, 53 men moonstruck; enemy's loss unknown.

The Ladysmith Bombshell.   69

Willie Illing, finding that the diminution of his wood pile near the Masonic Temple continued to an extraordinary extent, lay awake the other night in order to obtain, if possible, some clue to the mystery. At an hour when all honest folks should be in bed, hearing an operator at work in the yard, he cautiously slipped out by Colonel Stoneman's office and saw a lazy neighbour endeavouring to get a few heavy logs into a good-sized wheelbarrow. "You're a pretty fellow," said W. I., "to come and steal our contract wood while I sleep." "Yes," replied the visitor, "and you would stay there and see me break my back with lifting before you'd offer to come and help me!"

A Ladysmith friend of Mr. Kruger has received a letter stating that the old gentleman prayed for three hours the other night. He afterwards said he was perfectly happy. The Lord had told him to fight, and he was not afraid of General White.

THE SHELLS.

(With apologies to Edgar Allen Poe.)

Hear the shrieking of the shells—cursed shells;
What a host of Dutchmen their presence here foretells!
How they yell, and scream, and whistle at morning, noon, and
　　night—
　　　　While old Sol, who's hotly burning,
　　　　Smiles to see the people turning
　　　In a dickens of a fright,
　　　　　Keeping time, time, time,
　　　　　With the most infernal rhyme,
The shrieking and the screaming that so constantly foretells
Of the coming of the shells, shells, shells, shells,
Of the shrieking and the bursting of the shells.

See the little damage done—seldom done;
What a waste of powder : 'tis wasted by the ton !
How the Boers would storm and bluster, and be in a perfect fluster—
      Oh, what fun !
      Nothing done
    By the shells.
Though they come along in dozens, bringing sisters, aunts, and cousins,
They are practically harmless—those big shells.
Oh, the screaming of the shells, shells, shells ;
Oh, the shrieking and the bursting of the shells !

We are growing quite accustomed to the shells—
No one seems to mind their screaming and their yells ;
They may hiss, and shriek, and whistle at morning, noon, and night,
    While Old Sol keeps brightly shining
      On the citizens reclining
    In a state of calm delight,
Making fun all the time of that most infernal rhyme—
The shrieking and the screaming that so constantly foretells
Of the coming of the shells—the useless, futile shells ;
Of the shrieking and the bursting of the shells.

    Kit Harburn will not be happy till he gets one. He is now actively engaged making the seventh excavations with Garland's inside and out. Kit has had a few close shaves, but so far he is safe, and selling tickets for Phillips' next sweep.

    St. Jones' night was a convivial one, full justice being done to the champagne and whiskey. However, one little unfortunate occurrence happened towards midnight. One of the war correspondents mistook his way in the darkness, and found himself eventually lodged in the cells of the Police-station.

Annoyed at this, he made a tremendous noise by kicking the cell door with his heavy top boots. The genial C.C. going to the door, opened it a little, and said : " Man, ye micht pit aff your boots, an' I'll have them a bit rub, so that ye'll be respectable like when ye come up before Mr. Giles in the morning." The correspondent, flattered at the request, at once complied, and saw his mistake when Mr. MacDonald shut the door upon him, saying coolly, " Ye can kick awa' noo, my man, as lang as ye like."

Why is the Ladysmith army like a lady's skirt? Because it is hemmed in.

Mr. Farquhar has sent a very cordial invitation to Paul Kruger, asking him to attend the forthcoming function of the reopening of the railway to the Transvaal, and it is anticipated we shall soon have his honour in our midst again. It is nearly nine years since Paul came to us ; there was a great stir made upon the occasion and an address of welcome was presented upon the occasion ; the words were as follows : " To his Honour S.J.P.K., Knight Commander of the Legion of Honour, etc. We, as representing the inhabitants of the town, beg most heartily to welcome your honour on your visit to Ladysmith. We regret that your stay is of necessity of short duration.

" We are fain to hope that the visit of your honour will tend to more firmly cement the friendship which already exists between the burghers of your state and the inhabitants of this colony, trusting that your honour and the state you represent may enjoy many years of peace, happiness, and prosperity.— Signed, etc."

Ruddy Kipling Phillips is about the only man in town who has not taken shelter from the shells. He heeds them not. Three times daily he wends his way to the Crown corner.

Kip. is dejected at the closed doors, and consoles himself by whistling the old ditty, "Sweet spirit, hear my prayer." A little more patience, Kippy.

Orderly Officer (to Carbineers at dinner) : "Any complaints?" "Yis, sorr; the mate's all bone, sorr."

Harry Sparks, the M.L.A., has come up to Ladysmith to further enquire into the Asiatic question. He finds the town full of them, and feels himself bound to take immediate action. He is inducing the Mayor to convene a public meeting, and has already prepared a carefully-worded speech for the occasion.

The Natal Carbineer Sports are being held to-day under the distinguished shadow of Lombard's Kop and Umbulwana There is a long and varied programme; music is being supplied by Long Tom, Slim Pete, Baby Jack, Boys in Blue, Big Ben, and a host of others.

Enquiry Office for Missing Friends; office hours from dark to sunrise; fees, a fragment of shell from Long Tom or Silent Susan.

NOTICE.

As we find it impossible to send a separate reply to the numerous enquiries as to whereabouts of friends and relations, we publish for general information that—

> They've gone far away to a peaceful clime,
>   To get cured of their liver or bile;
> But where the foe lurks or the screaming shell bursts—
>   Not there, not there, my child.

Printed and Published at Ladysmith, Natal, 2 Dec., 1899.

NEVERMORE.

(With more apologies to E. A. Poe.)

Once upon a midnight dreary, while I pondered weak and weary,
Over all the quaint and curious yarns we've had about the war,
Suddenly there came a rumour (we can always take a few more),
Started by some chap who knew more than the others knew before—-
We shall have the Reinforcements in another—month or more :
      Only this, and nothing more.

But we're waiting still for Clery, waiting, waiting, sick and weary
Of the strange and silly rumours we have often heard before ;
And we now begin to fancy there's a touch of necromancy,
Something almost too unchancy in the undegenerate Boer :
      Only this, and nothing more.

Though our hopes are undiminished that the war will soon be finished,
We would be a little happier if we knew a little more ;
If we had a little fuller information about Buller,
News about Sir Redvers Buller and his famous Army Corps,
Information of the General and his fighting Army Corps:
      Only this, and nothing more.

And the midnight shells uncertain, whistling through the night's black curtain,
Thrills us, fills us, with a touch of horror never felt before ;
So that now to still the beating of our hearts we keep repeating,
'Tis some visitor entreating entrance at the chamber door,
Some late visitor entreating entrance at the chamber door :
      This it is, and nothing more.

Oh, how slow the shells come dropping, sometimes bursting,
    sometimes stopping—
As if they themselves were weary of the very languid war.
How distinctly we'll remember all the weary, dull November,
And it seems as though December will have little else in store,
And our Christmas dinner will be bully beef and plain stick-
    yaw:
                Only this, and nothing more.

Altham, Altham, tell us truly, if there's any news come newly,
Not the old fantastic rumours we have often heard before:
Desolate, yet all undaunted, in the town by Boers still haunted,
This is all the news that's wanted—tell us truly, we implore,
Is there, is there a relief force? Tell us, tell us, we implore:
                Only this, and nothing more.

For we're waiting rather weary. Is there such a man as Clery?
Are there really reinforcements? Is there any Army Corps?
Shall we see our wives and mothers, or our sisters and our
    brothers,
Shall we ever see those others who went southwards long before?
Shall we ever taste fresh butter? Tell us, tell us, we implore:
                Shall be answered nevermore.

"The man in the Balloon" is rightly judged to be one of the highest authorities on Ladysmith affairs, but even he does not profess to know everything, as evinced by the following set of queries he has sent us for solution. We will be sorry to receive replies.

    He is exceedingly anxious to know:

        Whether it is intended to publish a directory of the rabbit warrens, river bank, and of Funkemsdorp?

        Whether the former has not been declared a suburb of the latter?

Whether a good price would not be obtainable for a barrel of tar at Funkemsdorp?

Whether there is no scarcity of white feathers there?

Whether a search is on for a man who is quite a walking encyclopædia?

Whether an ex M. L. A. Wil-son return to Dundee?

THE SONG OF THE BESIEGED.

When Buller wheels round Lombard's Kop,
When Piet Joubert has done a "hop,"
We'll sing, if only over "dop,"
   "For this relief, much thanks!"

Of rations short we've had enough;
Of milk condensed quite "quantum suff.";
Of biscuit hard, and "bully" tough—
   "For this relief, much thanks"!

"Long Tom be hanged!" we bravely cry:
But when his shells go whizzing by,
And miss us—then we gently sigh,
   "For this relief, much thanks!"

To "Tom," "Big Ben," and "Silent Sue,"
To "Weary Willie," "Tired Tim," too,
We're ready quite to say "Adieu!"
   "For this relief, much thanks!"

When once again from flies we're freed,
When southwards merrily we speed,
Our "Mercury" and our "Witness" read—
   "For this relief, much thanks!"

When no more heard are " Who goes there ? "
" Of martial law are you aware ? "
And " Half-past eight ; lights out ; beware ! "
  " For this relief, much thanks."

And " Who are you ? " And " Where's your pass ? "
" Get out of this, you wretched ass ! "
" He-haw ! Hee-haw ! and my eye-glass ! "
  " For this relief, much thanks ! "

We know we've earned eternal fame :
But somehow—and just all the same—
We're all quite ready to exclaim :
  " For this relief, much thanks ! "

Dear Ladysmith ! Sweet, pretty thing,
Fond memories you'll ever bring ;
But please excuse us, while we sing—
  " For this relief, much thanks ! "

J. S. D.

Crowd at Post Office, reading " Latest " official information. Shell bursts somewhere in the neighbourhood, and one or two start at the sound. One of the crowd, cheerily : "Oh, it's only a shell." A laugh, and reading resumed.

A brilliant meteor passed from N. to S. the other evening, which caused no small alarm to the city watchers. No. 1 said the enemy was using rockets. No. 2 declared it was somebody signalling to the Boers, and called out the active guard from beneath the P. O. verandah. It might have been a shooting star, timidly suggested a listener ; or an infernal machine to destroy the town, chimed in another. " Oh, no," said No. 2, " I saw it with my own eyes. It was a lamp with several colours ; besides, don't you think I know a star when

I see it? Why, I've lived near Cape Town, where there is an observatory, and a fellow ought to know what a star is. We had better report the matter." Report made accordingly.

"Ha! Ha! this is splendid. Here's Pearce, he's risen from the dead." (Col. Rhodes).

The Convent is now empty. Nun left.

Sydney Thorrold appeared before the Magistrate this morning charged with committing an offence, viz., the displaying of lights after a certain hour in the store of Sparks Bros., on Saturday last. Mr. Thorrold pleaded guilty, and asked the Magistrate to take a lenient view, it being his first appearance. Col. Robert Walker and Capt. Bulleier, of the Town Guard, briefly stated the facts. The accused elected to give evidence, and informed the Bench that the lights were intended for Mr. S. W. Sutton's cat; he understood from Mr. Sutton that Mr. Marshall had arranged to send for them early in the evening; this, however, he neglected to do. Both Mr. Sutton and himself much regretted the occurrence, and they attached considerable blame to Mr. Marshall. Mr. Giles pointed out the absolute need of observing very carefully all orders and regulations issued during the siege. Without doubt the offence had been committed. He regretted he had no power to deal with Mr. Sutton or Mr. Marshall, but he ordered Mr. Thorrold to forthwith leave the town. (Mr. Thorrold, we understand, has now taken up his abode at Bellair.)

First Private: "Th' Captain told me to kape away from the inemy's foire." Second Private: "Phwat did ye till the Captain?" First Private: "I told him the Boers wus so busy shelling, they hadn't made any."

Messrs. Scott and Hyde, duly favoured with instructions from Mr. Lotter, will sell at his residence (or whatever is left of it) on Boxing Day, the whole remains of his household furniture and effects, including several fragments of a handsome wardrobe. Special terms to most purchasers. To Joubert and Co., terms strictly cash, etc.

THE HOME-COMING.

The flags unfurl! Beat loud the drums!
    Shout out the victor's song—
At last the day of triumph comes,
    For which we've waited long.
Yet while o'erhead bright garlands wave,
    And fragrant roses rain,
Forget we not those heroes brave
    Who'll ne'er come home again.

Hail! Lancers swift, and bold Dragoons!
    Leicesters and Rifles true!
Staunch Dublin lads; stern Gordon "loons";
    The gallant *Powerful's* crew.
Yet as ye march with heads upheld,
    A vacant place retain
For those whose graves are on the veld,
    Who'll ne'er come home again.

On! Volunteers—Natal's stout hearts!
    Light Horsemen of the Rand!
And all ye braves from many parts—
    A noble, conquering band.
But there were others fought and won;
    Yet they behind remain
To rest beneath the southern sun—
    They'll ne'er come home again.

Ye thousands, raise your deafening cheer
    As onward proud they go ;
But there are wives and mothers dear,
    And sires with locks of snow,
Who scan with tears the serried rows ;
    They look—but ah ! in vain—
To catch the longed-for smile of those
    Who'll ne'er come home again.

The vacant chair stands as it stood ;
    Fresh let their memory live !
Sweet life they gave for others' good—
    'Tis all a man can give.
They too were victors in the fray ;
    Then let us not restrain
A tear for those far, far away
    Who'll ne'er come home again.

In a recent copy of *The Diggers' News* it is announced that the Boer Government is actively engaged in the further development of the coal mines at Dundee and Elands Laagte. Supplies up to a reasonable quantity can be obtained free before the festive season sets in, upon names being communicated to the engineer in charge.

Mr. Colenbrander wishes his many friends to know that most of his young canaries have now left the nest ; he will be happy to supply pairs or single birds direct from Intomba, which climate he finds has a most detrimental effect upon the health and plumage of his choice songsters. Communication should be made to him forthwith, as he is leaving for Pretoria in the course of the next few days.

To Clear.—A large number of bath bricks and sugar-basins ; nothing else in stock. The establishment will be closed for the usual Christmas holidays. Apply, R. Graham (Ally's son).

IN THE FUTURE.

In Ladysmith, after the siege (which may reasonably be set down as having been raised in or about the year 1902).

Dramatis Personæ: Guileless Tourist, G. T.'s daughter, and Wily Guide.

Train arrives in the new palatial railway station.

G. T. and his daughter, alighting, are greeted with a chorus of "Guide, sir? All most interesting places pointed out, sir."

G. T. arranges with W. G. to view the ruins on following day.

G. T. (next day): Ah, this is—er—the Royal Hotel. What special interest—er—attaches to it?

W. G.: This way, sir, historical spot. Fifty-two shells went right through this room while fifty people were at lunch, sir. One shell landed in each of their plates, sir, but no one was hurt. Special dispensation, sir. Dr. Jameson stood just here, sir.

G. T.: But I—er—understood—er—that the doctor—er—lived in a—er—bomb-proof hole near his—er—house.

G. T.'s Daughter: Oh, how too awfully romantic!

W. G.: Just so, sir. But this special evening he ventured out after "cease firing" to collect shells.

G. T.: Oh, I see. What the *Bombshell* calls a—er—"Trogloditic Conchologoist"?

G. T. D.: A what, papa?

G. T. (with relish): A trogloditic conchologist, my dear.

W. G.: Just so, sir. Well, he came out, and was just drinking the last iced shandy procurable in town (he paid £5 5s.

for it, sir) when a shell came along from "Long Tom" and knocked the top of his glass, without spilling a drop.

G. T. D.: Oh, what a brave man. Did he finish the drink?

W. G.: Oh dear no, miss. He sold it at a loss to a friend in the bar, and cleared back to his cave.

G. T.: And these bits of rusty iron—er—guide?

W. G.: Oh, these, sir? Bits of the shells. Mr. Jones used to stroll about among them as they fell, and pick up the pieces. He has refused £2,000 for the collection. It brings him in an immense amount of custom. The other hotels, you see, sir, were practically out of it. The Sceptre was very slightly struck; and Barney, of the Station Hotel, had important business in Maritzburg just when the shelling came on. He cleared, sir, and has not been heard of since.

> There was an old man who took snough,
> Played a game that is usually called blough;
>   Britain took him in hand
>   (Took away, too, his land),
> Now do you not think that was rough?

A case which excited considerable interest was before the magistrate one day this week.

A military man who refused his name was charged with being drunk and incapable. He pleaded guilty

Magistrate to accused: Where did you obtain the liquor?

Accused: I can't remember, your worship

Magistrate to Chief Constable: Do you know Mr. Mac-Donald?

Chief Constable: No, sir.

Magistrate to Sergeant Miller: Do you know, Sergeant Miller?

Sergeant Miller: No, sir; only wish I did.

The accused was discharged.

If the relief column takes a day and a-half to march a yard and a-half, how much longer will the price of eggs be 10s. 7d. per dozen?

Notwithstanding the dryness of the season and the absence of the Indian Vegetable Hawker, the morning market prices are exceedingly moderate. We quote from Wednesday's return:—

Eggs	10s. 7d. per doz.
Tomatoes	0s. 4d. each.
New Potatoes	1s. 0d. per lb.
Vegetable Marrows	2s. 0d. each.
Carrots	3s. 0d. per bunch.
Cucumbers	3s. 6d. per brace.
Apples	5s. 0d. per small lot.

There was little or no demand for butter, forage, and firewood.

Other commodities outside the market are fetching reasonable prices: whiskey, any brand, £5 the bottle; condensed milk, 10s. a tin.

Wanted to know :—

> Whether the Boers have not formed a murderous idea to drive our troops to the horizon and over the edge? Whether this is not contrary to the Geneva Convention?
>
> If the *Powerful* is only waiting for a heavy dew to be able to get steam up for the relief of Ladysmith?

The Ladysmith Bombshell. 83

If Kruger has received the appointment of Governor of Britain's latest-acquired Colony?

How War Correspondents are to be distinguished from Camp-followers in the forthcoming battle; and whether they are likely to have the same influence as Bruce's memorable following at B—burn; and whether they are not as numerous as that following?

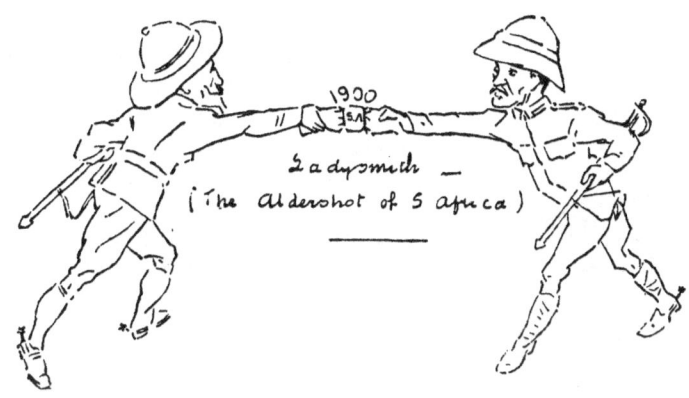

WHITE: Welcome, Sir Redvers: glad to see you here,
Although I cannot offer you the festive season's cheer.

BULLER: How do, Sir George? I'm sorry you have had to wait so long,
But Boers were thick as bumble-bees, and in position strong.

WHITE: Ah! well, our waiting's over: triumph's ours all 'long the line.

BULLER: Yes, I think our troubles ended with 1899.

MANY HAPPY RETURNS.

It was one of a procession of dhoolies carrying sick men to the hospital. The dhoolie was just like other dhoolies; the man just like other men; he had not taken a gun or won the Victoria Cross, yet the people crowded about him and jostled each other for a peep at him. The man was something more than a hero. "Who is he? What is he suffering from?" someone enquired. "He ain't suffering, mate," a corporal of the Devons replied; "he's the only really happy man in this camp. He's got delirium tremens."

A FRATRICIDAL WAR.

"Alas! war is a horrible thing," said the philosopher of Fort Funk. "Here we have the sad spectacle of brother slaughtering brother, just as though they were not of the same family." "Brother slaughtering brother!" exclaimed an astonished listener. "Yes," the philosopher went on; "didn't you hear that the Boers killed five mules in the artillery camp a few days ago."

THE SIX-INCH GUN.

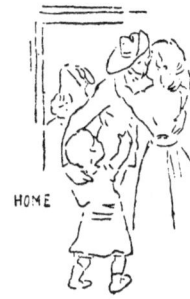

There is a famous hill looks down
Five miles away on Ladysmith town,
With a long flat ridge that meets the sky,
Almost a thousand feet on high,
    And on the ridge there is mounted one
    Long-range terrible six-inch gun.

And down in the street a bugle is blown
When the cloud of smoke on the sky is thrown,
For it's twenty seconds before the roar
Reverberates o'er, and a second more
    Till the shell comes down with a whiz and stun
    From that long-range terrible six-inch gun.

And men and women walk up and down
The long hot streets of Ladysmith town,
And the housewives work in the usual round,
And the children play till the warning sound,
    Then into their holes they scurry and run
    From the whistling shell of the six-inch gun.

For the shells they weigh a hundred pound,
Bursting wherever they strike the ground,
While the strong concussion shakes the air
And shatters the window-panes everywhere;
    And we may laugh, but there's little of fun
    In the bursting shell from a six-inch gun.

The Ladysmith Bombshell.

Oh! 'twas whistle and jest with the carbineers gay
As they cleaned their steeds at break of day,
But like a thunder-clap there fell
In the midst of the horses and men a shell—
    And the sight we saw was a fearful one,
    After that shell from the six-inch gun.

Though the foe may beset us on every side,
We'll find some cheer in this Christmas-tide;
We will laugh and be gay, but a tear will be shed,
And a thought be given to the gallant dead,
    Cut off in the midst of their life and fun
    By the long-range terrible six-inch gun.

    K now that the end draws nigh,
    R ash man, and thou must die!
    U seless resistance won't avail thee—
    G ermans, Frenchmen, all will fail thee;
    E asy times are nearly o'er :
    R evenge is Britain's, wily Boer.

Saturday morning.—It is reported this morning that a picket of the N.M.R. captured a Dutch General during the night's outpost duty. It seems there was an attempt to enter our lines, but the picket, being on the alert as usual, the enemy's plan was frustrated. The companions of the General succeeded in escaping, and the General himself was only secured with the greatest difficulty. The name of the General has not yet been ascertained.

Saturday afternoon.—It transpires that the capture effected by the N.M.R. picket last night was that of an old he-goat. In imagining that they had taken a Dutch General the N.M.R. were probably misled by the smell.

"How do you find the situation this morning, Thomas?"
"Find the situation, sir? why I lost mine two months ago."

The Ladysmith Bombshell.

Mr. Holliday, in his interesting "Dottings on Natal," written some thirty-five years ago, gives a brief account of Ladysmith. He thus describes the little Arcadia as he then found it. "Ladysmith, situated on a bend of the Klip River—a very dry spot. About fifteen years back a dam was erected across the river, at a heavy cost, to enable the town that was to be to obtain a supply of water; but the dam broke down, and the dammed water got away. One extra dry season an account was published in the newspapers stating that, as no water was obtainable, the inhabitants had to live on bottled beer. The buildings comprise about sixty houses, magistrate's office, gaol, chapel, and a gallows. Inhabitants 250."

The population now numbers 20,000 thirsty souls, with as many more waiting outside; the water is reported as unfit for "drinking purposes," and again the inhabitants will have reluctantly, perhaps, to fall back upon the "bottled beer."

A "Regular" "Royal" Christmas to us!
May our "Spirits" be unflagging, and
May Good Luck and Good Health
Be as loyal as the "United Service,"
   and
Go hand in hand to "Guard" us
In the coming year!

*Printed and Published at Ladysmith, Natal,
23 Dec., 1899.—G. W. L.*

MARKING TIME.

The New Year comes, so let us fill
The flowing bowl with right good-will,
Though Buller's at Colenso still
                Marking time.

We hoped—in human hopes we see
The idlest form of vanity ;
Ere this we should no longer be
                Marking time.

We dreamed of battles fought and won,
We dreamed our scattered foes would run
Before us—but we haven't done
                Marking time.

Our lingering faith is growing small :
"Where's Buller ? " is the weary call ;
Where's French ? Where's Clery ? They are all
                Marking time.

November passed ; we smiled and said
"Another week ! " that week soon sped ;
But still we smiled, "Next week." That fled.
                And we marked time.

The New Year comes, and we are here,
With every prospect still to fear
The dawning of another year—
                Marking time !

"One of the things that strikes me in connection with smoking," observes Harry Pearson, "is the fact that smokers, if out of tobacco, do not hesitate to ask another smoker for a pipefull or a cigarette, as the case may be. I have often

The Ladysmith Bombshell. 89

looked upon this as indicative of a lack of independence; I have felt that I would rather go without a smoke till I could obtain a supply of the weed—I mean, if I were a smoker. This is not stinginess on my part, for I have often kept, till the last few days, a packet of cigarettes in my pocket in order to be able to accommodate my friends."

[You are wrong, Mr. Pearson, in ascribing this to a want of independence. With smokers, as with many other communities of persons following the same trade or the same form of amusement or study, there is a kind of freemasonry. You feel no hesitation in asking a favour because you are always ready to do the same yourself. This fellowship is a potent factor for good, inasmuch as it induces and fosters kindliness towards our neighbour. Of course, one's good nature is sometimes abused. If people knew that you kept cigarettes for promiscuous distribution, you would find, at the present time, the expense of replenishing your stock pretty big.—ED.]

Mr. Tom Brookes is now gathering his ripe peaches (not for Dyson's Market, but for a few of his friends in the immediate neighbourhood). Some of them scale seventeen ounces each.

Whereas it has been reported to the Government that the British flag will be shortly hoisted at Pretoria, Notice is hereby given that all Burghers and true friends of the Republic are commanded, when the event happens, to take off hats and sing "Rule, Britannia." The day will be kept as a public holiday. (Extract from notice at Pretoria.)

THERE WAS AN OLD NIGGER, HIS NAME, ETC.

There is a white nigger, and they call him Piet Joubert,
  And his fighting's awfully slow;
Buller's coming up behind him, and it's very, very clear
  To the nether regions soon Joubert will go.

Chorus—So saddle up your horses, keep your rifles clean,
    Sling your cartridges around your manly chest ;
    Buller's men will do their share ; but it's easy to be seen
    That our garrison will have to do the rest.

Piet Joubert, he has no conscience—he's an awful, awful skunk—
On our sick and on our wounded he has fired ;
But, judging from the symptoms, it is plain he's in a funk—
" Long Tom " and " Big Ben " are growing very tired.
    Chorus—So saddle, etc.

But in fighting with true Britons he is dealing with brave men,
    Who will never, never strike below the belt ;
They will fight on lines humane, though outnumbered ten times ten ;
    They'll fight fair, however angry they have felt.

Chorus—So saddle up your horses, and go in to fight,
    Like true Britons, ever ready for the fray ;
    Strike 'em hard, but strike 'em fair ; on our side we have the right,
    And grand victory will crown that glorious day.

It is reported that the members of the Town Guard who so smartly out-manœuvred the Boers by evacuating the town before it was invested, are now anxious to return in time to take part in the approaching peace celebrations.

    B uller, Buller, hear our loud entreaty,
    U nder dire bombardment we are laid ;
    L et thy legions come to us in pity,
    L et them come, and lend us all thy aid.
    E ndurance has been tried, and stood the test right well,
    R elieve and aid us ; oh, hear the besiegers yell.

The Ladysmith Bombshell.   91

The Mayor: I am afraid there is nothing in the way of work to give you just now; there is very little to do.

Refugee: That's just the kind of work I enjoy, sir.

After sixty days' siege it is of little wonder that people are not eager to know the time of day. One occasionally meets with the enquiry, "Let me see, to-day is——." In the future the question will be, "What month are we in now?" To remedy this perplexing state of affairs, and to satisfy all manner of doubt, there has been a sharp run on pocket-knives, and the thoughtful inhabitant is carefully "notching" each day on his walking-stick. It is surmised he will require a good many of these sticks before the difficulty is over.

Mems.—30th December, 1880: South African Republic proclaimed. 1st January, 1896: Dr. Jameson's catastrophe.

Extract *Standard and Diggers' News.*—£1,000 Reward.— Whereas on the night of the 18th December last some evil-disposed person or persons did wilfully destroy and carry away certain heavy guns from Lombard's Kop, Natal, the said guns being the property of the Z.A.R., anyone giving information that will lead to the recovery of the guns and to the punishment of the offenders will be rewarded as above.—Apply, etc.

The C squadron of the N.M.R., known as the "Forty Thieves," have formed a band. By kind permission of the officers they will perform on the Market Square this evening. Each item on the programme will be performed with variations. A prize of £1 1s. will be given by Mr. Allsopp to any member of the audience identifying any particular air.

Captain Molyneux is having a good deal of anxiety with regard to the outfit of the members of the Town Guard. By dint of much perseverance a supply of Madagascar meat and bread is now obtained at 6 o'clock in the morning; but the genial captain is not satisfied with this, and the order now goes forth that the "watchers on the Klip are from the beginning of the year to wear kilts, as owing to the extreme dampness of the ground the men's trousers have so considerably shrunk as to make it impossible to get their feet through."

Regret.—One of the Naval Brigade was removing a fuse from a live shell when it exploded, carrying away his left arm. "Well, that is too bad," exclaimed he, "for it was only yesterday that I paid 10s. for having that same arm tattooed."

THE CIVILIAN'S COMPLAINT.

Who made a mess of this 'ere war?
Who dilly-dallied from afar?
And left us in this "nasty jar"? . . .

Who told us when this siege begun
Our enemies right soon should run?
(Upon my word, it takes the bun.) . . .

Who was't that told us to provide
Ten days of rations, so's to tide
Us over Joubert's monstrous stride? . . .

Who then swooped town, and commandeered
All stores, when famine once was feared,
And left us all to "dree our weird"? . . .

Who recks not if we live or die?
Who will not let us victuals buy?
Although the stores can yet supply? . . .

Who has the best of this affair?
We citizens who live on air?
Nay, we're worse off than our bugbear—
    The en-em-y.

Thanks to Woodhouse, and Frank Reed, too,
They get us beef eno' to stew :
Some people make a great ado—
    'Tis tough, they say.

Let Buller come or Buller stop,
We'll stick this show out till we drop,
And never leave this blessed shop,
    Though bad it be.

We'll stay to see the fighting o'er ;
If needs be, we will do our share ;
And then we'll advertise galore
The hard times we have had to bear.
We'll slate Great Britain right and left ;
We'll curse the British Parliament.
Of friends and property bereft,
We'll show to all the world we meant
To demonstrate the sad delay
That's caused our misery to-day.
    Confound J— C. !

It was a wet, drenching day. The Carbineers had been in the saddle some four or five hours. An order was issued from headquarters that, on returning from duty, the men were to change their shirts ; so the Captain sent for the Sergeant and gave the order. "But, sir," said the Sergeant, "the men have only one apiece left." "No matter," replied Capt. Molyneux "they must change with each other."

  When freends frae freends are gaun to part,
  An' parting causes mony a smart,
  A wee, wee drap cheers up the heart
    And mak's them pairt fu' frisky O.

And when returned—been absent lang,
And absence brings them mony a pang—
Their joys maun hae an auld Scot's sang,
  Wi' a drap o' Hielant whisky O.

A drap o' barley bree sae clear,
It droons oor care an' flags oor fear,
Mak's freends and Dutch like brithers dear,
  A drap o' Hielant whisky O.

WHAT NEWS?

What news? what news? what anxious ones are waiting
  Far off to know if with us all is well!
What news? what news? with pulses palpitating,
  They wait and hope, for there is none to tell.

What news? what news? Oh, anxious one, thou fearest
  To listen yet for what may give thee pain.
What news? what news? Perchance thy best and dearest
  Will never clasp thee to his heart again.

What news? what news? What homes are desolated!
  What mothers' hearts must sorrow evermore;
What loving ones can never now be mated;
  What constant vows no more be whispered o'er.

What news? what news? Perhaps no more, hereafter,
  Thy friend will meet thee with a smile;
No more thy heart shall echo to the laughter
  Of happy children whom thou lovedst erewhile.

What news? what news? Are not the hosts engaging
  In some fierce conflict under the sun's glare?
What news? what news? What battles then are raging
  'Mid rocky hills? What streams are reddened there?

What news? what news? Our leader, hath he left us,
   And shall his voice no longer call us on?
Too well we know that fate hath thus bereft us;
   That voice is silenced and Harry Escomb gone.

What news? what news? Still in the balance pending
   The right and wrong—the future that will be.
What news? what news? with hopes and fears unending,
   Yet strong and steadfast till the victory.

"There is a man in the front room wants to see you, Mr. Banbery." Mr. Banbery: "I'll be there in a minute; ask him to take a chair." "He says he's going to take them all; he's from the military authorities, I fancy."

The Umbrella Hospital, Ladysmith.—Fractured ribs and dislocated joints scientifically mended and set by an eminent professor; debilitated frames revived and strengthened, and recovery guaranteed while you wait.

THE COUNTERSIGN.

Captain Bulleier (of the Town Guard) generally has some difficulty in making out the orders. The other wet night he was placed on sentry duty near Matthew Brown's (the usual smelling-bottle not being omitted). After awhile, Adjutant Brandon visited him and enquired what would be the first thing to do if the enemy were to surprise him. "I'd get the countersign, sir." "But they are the enemy, and don't know it," said the Adjutant. "Well, sir, I'd make them repeat it after me till they did know it, and if that didn't succeed, I'd get Brother Dunkley to let fly with his rifle."

"A WARRIOR BOLD AM I."

It will be generally conceded that a few of the officers of our Volunteer forces have a very good idea of their own importance; and it is a well-known fact that an impression is ingrained in these few that their personal comfort and convenience are items of the utmost importance to the final success of the present campaign. There is an old proverb concerning the destination of a beggar when mounted on a pegasus; but surely a worse fate will be provided for the volunteer officer when astride of his high horse " Self-conceit." Certain of these gentlemen have the good fortune to be quartered in a garden adjoining a residence where a very tiny dog is kennelled, who does his utmost to earn his food by acting as a small watch-dog, giving vent to occasional immature barks, the best he can produce, poor little mite, as a warning against intruders. A native servant was sent by his master to ask that the dog might be destroyed, as its barking disturbed his slumbers. Just imagine an officer, living on premises by courtesy of the owner, actually requesting that a dog belonging to that owner should be made away with, because its barking annoyed its officership. Here we have a " Soldier of the Queen," used to the hurtle and bruit of battle, accustomed to bivouac in the open, actually unable to sleep because of the yelping of that wee, tiny dog, whose only fault is that he does his duty.

> " Oh, wad some power the giftie gie us
> Tae see oorsels as ithers see us."

Wilson's Music and General Printing Co., Ltd., 67b, Turnmill St., London.

www.ingramcontent.com/pod-product-compliance
Lightning Source LLC
Chambersburg PA
CBHW032131090426
42743CB00007B/560